Welcome to the BIG Academy

12 BIG Questions

Exploring God's Story

A 12 SESSION RESOURCE FOR USE WITH CHILDREN AGED 7-11

First published in 2013 by Elevation
Elevation is part of Memralife Group, registered charity number 1126997,
a company limited by guarantee, registered in England and Wales,
number 6667924. 14 Horsted Square, Uckfield, East Sussex, TN22 1QG

British Library Cataloguing in Publication Data

A catalogue record for this book is available from the British Library

ISBN 978-1-899788-92-7

Cover Design: Dan Armstrong at Wildfire Studio
Illustration: Dave Gray
Design: Beatroot Media and Steve Squires
Printed by Saxoprint

CONTENTS

THE CONCEPT AND OPENING SESSION

The idea of this 12 week 'course' is that it is the BIG Academy for your 7-11s group.

The 12 weeks should help them to feel equipped, ready and trained to go and change the world for Jesus!

The opening track on the '*Welcome to the BIG Academy*' CD is the theme song, and we recommend you use this at every session. This will give continuity and then they'll really get to know it. In our experience it quickly becomes a favourite. (There are actions ready for you to learn on the BIG Ministries website: www.bigministries.co.uk).

Each of the sessions is based around one of the songs from '*Welcome to the BIG Academy*'. We have included the song as part of the programme for the session as it fits really well! Doing a new song every week is a challenge, so don't feel you have to sing the song the session is based around. You could do a favourite of your group instead, or listen to the recommended track rather than singing it. We would recommend doing at least one song within each session.

The BIG Academy

It's very exciting for children to see that they are part of something BIG, and part of something that can actually make a difference. We believe that the children you are working with can really change the world for Jesus. That's why we want to inspire you to make this BIG Academy as exciting as you can for the children, and really start to get them excited about this.

Induction Session

We recommend having a session prior to the beginning of the 12 weeks where the children can come and have a whole lot of fun 'enrolling' onto the Academy, including getting their ID badges and Special Agent names!

Here are some ideas for you to do this. We would even recommend doing this in an evening before you start week 1 - make it super special!

4 weeks before:
Send out invites to the children to their BIG Academy Induction Evening. Here's a possible wording for you:

Dear Future BIG Academy Agent [insert child's name].

You have been specially selected to attend the BIG Academy.
In 12 weeks we will train you to go and change the world in Jesus' name.

You are required to attend the induction to the BIG Academy

On [insert date and time].
Location [insert location].

This message will self-destruct in 5 seconds... (not really, but it sounded good, huh?)

Things to do in your induction:

1) **ID Photo.** Set up a white background ready for the children to stand in-front of. When they arrive, stand them in-front of the screen and take their photo. Tell them this is for their ID card.

2) **Top Secret Special Agent Packs.** Have a pack ready for each of the children as soon as they have had their photo taken.

Brown envelopes with a TOP SECRET stamp on the outside look brilliant. (You can buy a TOP SECRET stamp online - I think it might be worth getting one as I'm sure it'll come in handy!)

In their pack include the following (as well as anything else you think might be suitable/fun!):

- little black notebooks with TOP SECRET stamped on the outside
- pens (you could get some colour-changing 'magic pens')
- their own Special Agent name (using a Code Breaker like the one below to de-cypher the name)
- magnifying glass
- Bible (if you have the budget to buy them!)
- lanyard (for their ID badges when they are made)
- popping candy (with a DANGER EXPLOSIVES label stuck on it)

Ideas for Special Agent names:

Black Thorn
Silent Bear
Stealth Sloth
Slate Turtle
Neon Pony
Ruby Snake
Diamond Lizard
Silver Ninja
Blue Bomber
Green Tiger

Hopefully that'll give you enough to think up some of your own! You could even think up specifically catered names for your group.

Code Breaker

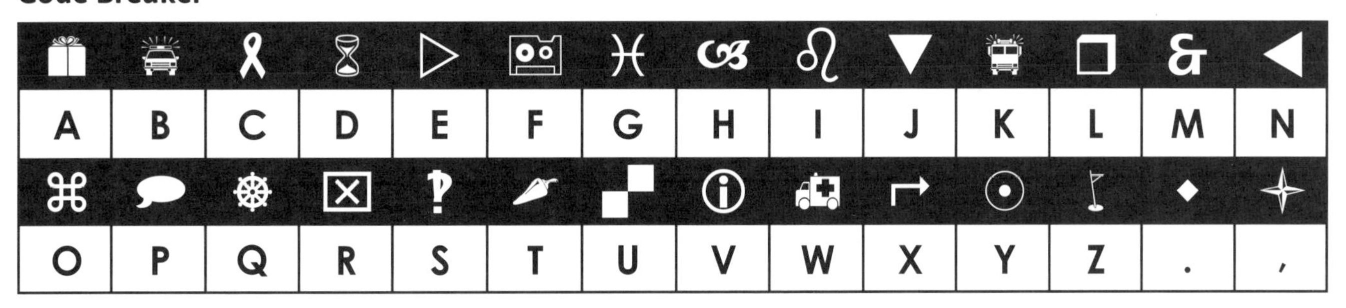

3) **Have a visit from a 'Top Special Agent'.** Someone who can come in and talk about doing things for Jesus - how the 'training' helped them; what they are doing to change the world for Jesus? Get the children to ask them questions.

There are a few ways that you can make this really cool if you have the time/know-how.

a) Get some walkie-talkies and have the Top Special Agent in the building, but you can't see him/her - to protect his/her identity of course!
b) Video the Top Special Agent and have him/her on-screen in front of the children. You could even black out his/her face - to protect his/her identity again...
c) If there is an internet connection, you could even do a Skype call and have a mock mission-style background behind the Top Special Agent.

Be as creative as you can and make it as 'special-agent-ish' as you can (time and budget allowing!).

The Top Special Agent could even teach the children the BIG Academy theme song. (Track 1 on *Welcome to the BIG Academy*.) If not, make sure you teach this at some point!

4) **Play some games**

Observational skill training
Put a number of objects on a tray and give the children one minute to look at it, then take it away. Remove a few of the items and put it back and then get the children to write down what they think has gone missing.

Hunt the verse
Use a QR Code Generator (*or use paper for a tech-free version!*) and create clues for the children to follow in order to find pieces of the Bible verse (and sweets!). They have to collect all of the 'pieces' and then put it together to complete the challenge and find the Bible verse. We suggest printing out the verse then cutting it up into a jigsaw. QR Code Generator here: *http://www.classtools.net/QR/* (these QR codes are just text based, so no internet is required. You will need at least one smart phone with a QR code reader on it though). Bible verse: Isaiah 6:8 'Then I heard the voice of the Master: Who shall I send? Who will go for us?' I spoke up: 'I'll go. Send me!'

Laser course
If you have a 'corridor' space this is perfect. But it would be possible in a 'normal' room. You could even use tables to create a 'corridor'. Attach red ribbon/wool to both walls in a 'laser maze' fashion. The challenge for the children is to get through without touching any of the 'lasers'. Here's a picture of a complicated one - you can go a lot simpler than this and it will still be fun!

5) **Have some food together**.

Tell the children next time you meet you'll have their ID badges ready, and that they should bring their notebooks and pens ready to get started at The BIG Academy.

BIG Question #1

WHEN SHOULD WE PRAISE GOD?

The Song:

BRAND NEW DAY

You will need:

6 mins

- Party music and facilities to play it!
- Pass the Parcel (optional)

Play a party game. Pass the parcel or musical statues would be good.
Have some fun; make it feel like a real celebration!

You will need:

4 mins

- A giant present
  On the gift tag it should read, 'for you'. Inside, place a large piece of paper with the day and date of the session written at the top. (Make it look like a page of a diary, with some entries like: 1030 - Church, 1300 - Lunch, 1600 - Homework! Make the entries relevant to the age of your group.)

Set the scene

Tell the children that the BIG Question we're thinking about today is:
When should we praise God?

Ask the children what they think.

Get the children to open the present.
[Warning: they will most likely be disappointed!]

Tell the children this

God gives us every day to live. It's a bit weird to think of every day as a present, but that's what it is! Psalm 118 says: "This is the day that the Lord has made, let us rejoice and be glad in it!" So we should do our best to praise God every day, because God has made every day for us.

(Optional) **You will need:**

7 mins

- A piece of A4 paper for every child in your group. Each piece of paper must have one of the days, Monday to Sunday, written on it (making sure every day is included)
- Pens
- Ribbon/wrapping paper
- Glue and scissors

Give the children a 'day' each. Get them to decorate the days so that every day looks like a present. Reminding them that every day is a gift for them from God.

and

13 mins

You will need:

- Story script (starting on *page 11*)
- Dressing-up clothes (optional)
- *Welcome to the BIG Academy* album (Track 2) and facilities to play it.
- Rhythm instruments (optional)

Teach the children the trigger words and encourage them to interact as you tell them the story.

All the children are going to be part of this story. So you need to choose:

- one person to be Paul
- one person to be Silas
- one person to be the jailer
- Everyone else will be the other prisoners

As you read the narration, encourage the children to follow along and act it out, even repeating any character's lines after you have read them.

We have incorporated a couple of additional elements/interludes in the story too:

- The song *Brand New Day* is used as the song the prisoners sing to praise God
- There will also be a noisy interlude for the earthquake. You can do this however you wish to; stomping/clapping/using rhythm instruments - just make lots of noise!

10-13 mins

You will need:

- An activity sheet copied for each child
- Pens/pencils
- Bibles

Go through the sheet - use it as a foundation for discussion. Allow the children to do the sheet however they would like to, but talk to them about the key questions as they are doing things.

5-10 mins

You will need:

- Paper and pens
- Card frames and stickers/decorations (optional)
- Copies of a prayer that you've written in bubble writing for colouring in (optional)

Write a short prayer together (or get the children to do it individually) to say in the mornings.

Alternatively, give the children a copy of a prayer you've written to colour/decorate. It should be a short prayer that praises God and thanks Him for the Brand New Day that is about to start.

OPTIONAL
You could write them up nicely and make frames/laminate them so the children can stick them up by their bed, somewhere they will see it every morning.

So... when should we praise God?
Every day!

PAUL & SILAS IN PRISON (ACTS 16:25-40)

TRIGGER WORDS **Smelly:** "Poooey!"
Rejoice/rejoiced/rejoicing: "WOOO-HOOO!"

Locked away from the rest of the world, away from their friends and family, not knowing if they would ever get out, Paul and Silas sat in the dark, damp, cold and **smelly** prison, watching spiders creep around and mice and rats scurry along the filthy stone floor. Other prisoners grumbled and moaned. Some of them had been down there for a long time - murderers, thieves, liars and cheats. They were all there.

But what were Paul and Silas doing there? They didn't belong in prison. They had done nothing wrong. What were they going to do?

They could've moaned like all of the other prisoners... but they didn't do that.

They could've got really angry and shouted and argued with one another... but they didn't do that.

They could've tirelessly started hacking away at the chains that were fixed tightly to their ankles and attempted a dramatic and daring escape... but they did not do that either.

Paul and Silas, amidst the darkness of the prison and with all of the other prisoners listening, began singing. They **rejoiced**! They sang songs to praise God and they prayed. Can you believe it!? In what seemed to be one of the worst situations they could find themselves in, they praised God. They **rejoiced**.

[SING IT! - Track 2 - BRAND NEW DAY]

It was dark, it was damp, it was cold and it was **smelly**. Paul and Silas sat in prison watching spiders creep around and mice and rats scurry along the filthy stone floor.

It was now midnight and, as Paul and Silas continued singing praises to God and **rejoicing**, something very unexpected happened... It began with a deep rumbling sound; then things began to rattle and shake - The walls, the floor, the gates, the chains... everything! Everything was shaking! The rattling and rumbling and the shaking quickly became more and more ferocious! It was... AN EARTHQUAKE!

[MAKE THE NOISE OF AN EARTHQUAKE]

The earthquake shook the prison so much that all of the prisoners' chains fell off and all of the doors of the jail cells flew open.

But Paul and Silas did not use this as an opportunity to escape from the dark, damp, cold, **smelly** prison. They stayed right where they were.

However, in the commotion, and in the darkness of the dungeons, the jailer appeared.

"Oh no!", said the very worried jailer, "the prison gates are all open. All of the prisoners must've escaped!"

Thinking that he was going to be in more trouble than he could bear to face, the jailer reached for his sword, ready to kill himself! But Paul, seeing what was happening, quickly jumped to his feet and shouted...

"STOP! You're not going to be in trouble! We're all still here. Look for yourself."

And when the jailer looked around, he saw that it was just as Paul said. Not one of the prisoners had escaped. They were all still there in the dark, damp, cold, **smelly** prison - watching spiders creep around and mice and rats scurry along the filthy, and now shattered, stone floor...

That very night, after all that had happened, the jailer's life changed as he believed in Jesus. He was baptised, along with his whole family and he took Paul and Silas to his house for dinner. Because he now believed in Jesus, they all **rejoiced**!

The next day Paul and Silas were released from the dark, damp, cold **smelly** prison. They then went and told their friends about all of the amazing things that had happened. Together, they **rejoiced**.

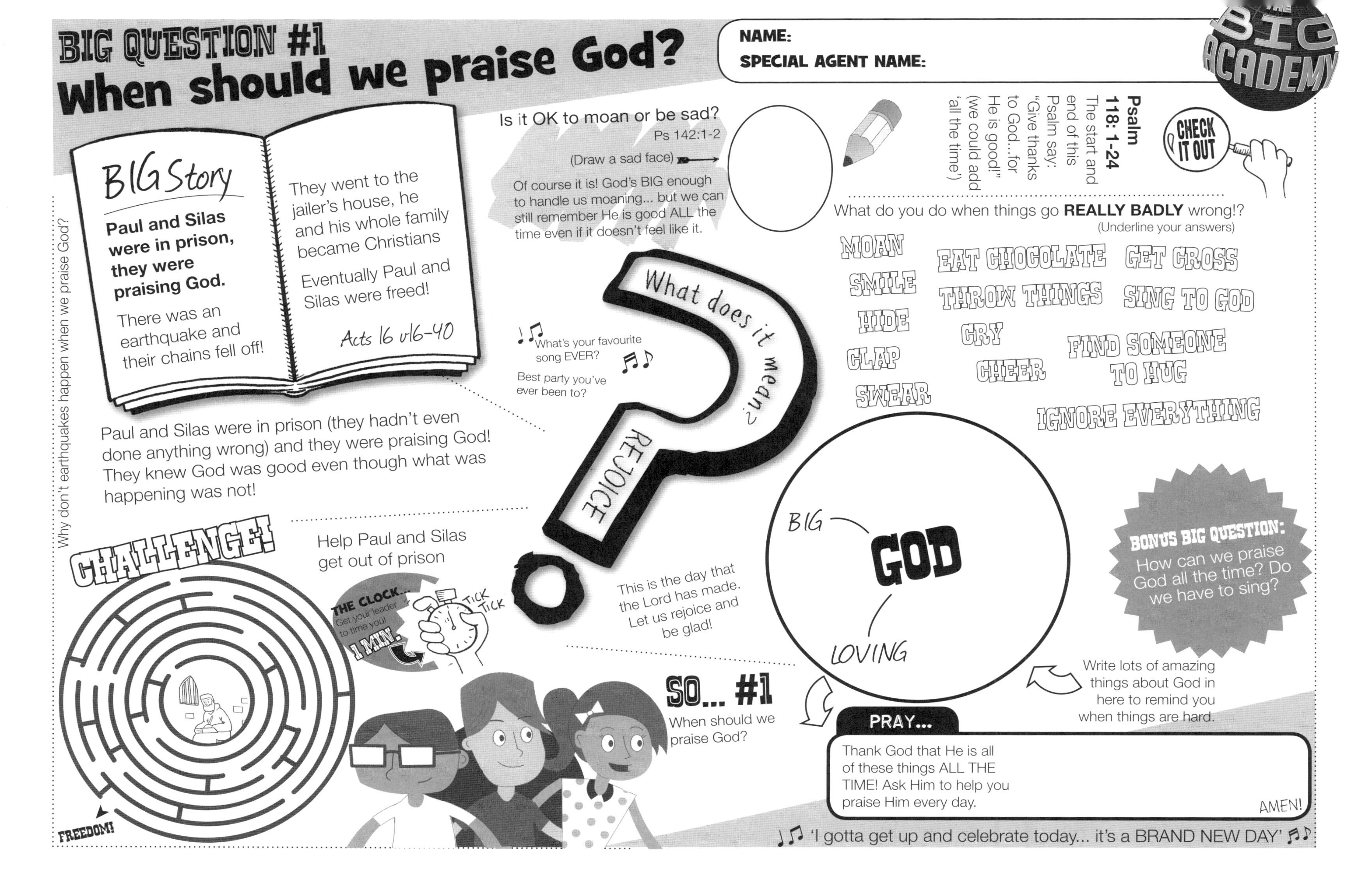
BIG QUESTION #1
When should we praise God?
NAME:
SPECIAL AGENT NAME:
THE BIG ACADEMY
BIG Story
Paul and Silas were in prison, they were praising God.
There was an earthquake and their chains fell off!
They went to the jailer's house, he and his whole family became Christians
Eventually Paul and Silas were freed!
Acts 16 v16-40
Paul and Silas were in prison (they hadn't even done anything wrong) and they were praising God! They knew God was good even though what was happening was not!
Is it OK to moan or be sad?
Ps 142:1-2
(Draw a sad face)
Of course it is! God's BIG enough to handle us moaning... but we can still remember He is good ALL the time even if it doesn't feel like it.
CHECK IT OUT
Psalm 118: 1-24
The start and end of this Psalm say: "Give thanks to God...for He is good!" (we could add 'all the time')
What do you do when things go REALLY BADLY wrong!?
(Underline your answers)
MOAN
SMILE
HIDE
CLAP
SWEAR
EAT CHOCOLATE
THROW THINGS
CRY
CHEER
GET CROSS
SING TO GOD
FIND SOMEONE TO HUG
IGNORE EVERYTHING
What does it mean?
REJOICE
What's your favourite song EVER?
Best party you've ever been to?
This is the day that the Lord has made. Let us rejoice and be glad!
BIG
GOD
LOVING
BONUS BIG QUESTION:
How can we praise God all the time? Do we have to sing?
Write lots of amazing things about God in here to remind you when things are hard.
SO... #1
When should we praise God?
PRAY...
Thank God that He is all of these things ALL THE TIME! Ask Him to help you praise Him every day.
AMEN!
'I gotta get up and celebrate today... it's a BRAND NEW DAY'
CHALLENGE!
Help Paul and Silas get out of prison
THE CLOCK...
Get your leader to time you!
1 MIN.
TICK TICK
FREEDOM!
Why don't earthquakes happen when we praise God?

BIG Question #2

DID GOD MAKE ME?

The Song:

WONDERSTRUCK

5-8 mins

You will need:

- Play-dough (recipe below to make it at home!)
- Cards with the names of items on that the children can make out of play-dough (two identical sets of 10)

Play a quick game of *Make It!* Split the children into two teams and give each team a lump of play-dough.

It will be a race to guess all 10 items on the cards. Give one child from each team the first card to do. Once the group have guessed it, another member of the team can come and get the next card. The first group to complete all 10 are the winners.

Recipe for play-dough:

- 2 cups flour
- 1 cup salt
- 2 cups water
- 2 tablespoons oil
- 2 teaspoons cream of tartar
- Few drops of food colouring (you can even add glitter if you want!)

Cook mixture in a pan over a medium heat, stirring all the time to prevent sticking.

Remove from the heat when mixture comes away from the sides of the pan.

Knead and store in an airtight container (it will keep for ages like this).

5 mins

You will need:

- Ink pads (preferably washable/non-toxic!)
- Paper (printed with five small squares for the 'fingerprints')
- Wet wipes!
- Magnifying glass (optional)

Set the scene:

Get everyone to do a set of prints of their fingerprints. Make the process as similar to a 'crime-lab' as you can. Compare the prints making sure the print is of the entire fingertip and then use the magnifier to look at the patterns.

Talk about the fact that every single person in the world (approx. 7 billion people) has a totally unique set of fingerprints. There has never been anyone with the same prints as you, and there never will be!

Get the children to title their page: 'I am unique' (you may need to explain what unique means!). Tell the children that the BIG Question we're thinking about today is: *Did God make me?*

You will need:

10 mins

- Story script (starting on *page 16*)
- Dressing-up clothes/junk/action figures/anything else you can think of that can be used to create the days of creation! (optional)

Divide the children into two groups (or keep them all together if it's a small group)

Tell them that whenever they hear the line, 'What on earth did it look like?' they are to create, as best they can, whatever they think the day looked like, using whatever materials you give them.

Give them a time limit for each 'day'. You could even make it a competition and award points.

You will need:

5 mins

- *Welcome to the BIG Academy* album and facilities to play it.

Sing *Wonderstruck* together (Track 3).

You will need:

10-13 mins

- An activity sheet copied for each child
- Pens/pencils
- Bibles

Go through the sheet - use it as a foundation for discussion. Allow the children to do the sheet however they would like to, but talk to them about the key questions as they are doing things.

(Optional) **You will need:**

8 mins

- Origami paper (or squares of paper that you've made)
- Pens
- Instructions from: http://en.origami-club.com/easy/index.html

There are loads of 'easy' origami patterns on this website. Go here and choose one or two that you think you and the children you are with could make. Print out the instructions, practise making it and then make it with the children!

Get the children to stand up and teach them this 'chant'.

3 mins

Ask them to repeat each line after you. (If you have an older group, they will be able to remember it and could put all 3 lines together without your intervention each time!)

God made me	('God' - point to the sky; 'me' - point to yourself)
God made you	('God' - point to the sky; 'you' - point to someone else)
God is amAAAAzing!	('God' - point to the sky, 'amAAAAzing' get them to think of a big action)

CREATION (GENESIS 1 - 2:1-3)

What was there in the beginning? Where were we? Where were the animals, plants, trees and oceans? The sky, even? I'll tell you - they were nowhere to be seen! They were non-existent! They had not yet been formed. No one had made them; no one had moulded or sculpted the mountains and landscapes; no one had spoken them into existence. At this point, there was nothing! Only God...

But... What on earth did this look like?

All of this was to change. God spoke. From the immediacy of God's command, the most spectacular light appeared out of nothing. God caused the light to be separated from the darkness. The light would be called day; the darkness was to be called night. Morning, afternoon, evening and night happened for the very first time. So that was that. That was the first day.

But... What on earth did it look like?

Have you looked out your window and seen the sky lately? The massive blue space up above holding the puffy, swirly, and brush stroked clouds of infinite shapes and sizes, all floating around beyond our reach. Where were they in the beginning? They were nowhere to be seen... Until God spoke! And the seas and oceans, what about them? That's a lot of buckets of water! But where were they in the beginning? They were nowhere to be seen... Until God spoke! So that was that. That was the second day.

But... What on earth did it look like?

Mmmm food. What's your favourite fruit or vegetable? Can you imagine if they never existed!? If you were never able to experience the taste of an apple or drink orange juice? What if potatoes never happened? No chips, crisps or mash and gravy! Where were they in the beginning? They were nowhere to be seen!... Until God spoke!

And flowers and trees, what about them? Tiny, pretty petaled flowers and trees in which to climb and shade ourselves from the sun; where were they in the beginning? They were nowhere to be seen... Until God spoke! So that was that. That was the third day.

But... What on earth did it look like?

Spring, Summer, Autumn or Winter - what's your favourite time of the year? All the different colours and weather that comes with each season; where did they come from? Where were they in the beginning? The sun, moon and stars shining high and bright for all to see... Unless it's cloudy, of course... But, where were they in the beginning? They were nowhere to be seen.... Until God spoke! So that was that. That was the fourth day.

But... What on earth did it look like?

If you'd never seen a bird would you ever dream about flying? Flapping wings and pointy beaks all soaring in every direction across the skies. "Chirp-chirp! Caw-caw! Twit-twoo!" But where were they in the beginning? They were nowhere to be seen!... Until God spoke!

And where would Captain Birdseye be if there were no fish in the waters? Think of the huge whales guarding the oceans; the crabs and other crustaceans; the colourful fish of the tropical seas, jellyfish and other weird and bizarre shaped creatures that lie on the murky ocean depths? Where did they come from? Where were they in the beginning? They were nowhere to be seen... Until God spoke! So that was that. That was the fifth day.

But... What on earth did it look like?

Listen up a minute. I'm not finished yet! How would you know if you were a 'cat person or a dog person' if you'd never ever seen one? What about - monkeys, cows, mice and star-nosed moles to name but a few - all of these animals that walk and climb amongst the rocks and fields and trees of the earth. Where were they in the beginning? They were nowhere to be seen... Until God spoke!

And what about you!? What about me!? What about your friends; your family? Where did it all start? How did we get here? Where were we in the beginning? We were nowhere to be seen... Until God spoke! So that was that. That was the sixth day.

But... What on earth did it look like?

God then took a day to relax and to look at the magnificence of all He'd created as He walked amongst it and held it in His hands. So... that was that. That was the seventh day.

Now... What did that look like?

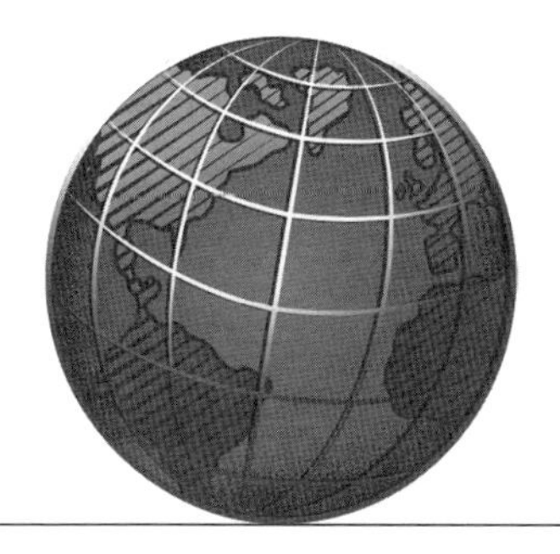

BIG QUESTION #2
Did God make me?
NAME:
SPECIAL AGENT NAME:
THE BIG ACADEMY
BIG Story
There was nothing...
God made everything!
It was good.
God rested.
Genesis 1+2
What's the best thing you've ever made?
What's your favourite bit of creation?
DRAW IT HERE:
CHECK IT OUT
Psalm 139:13-14
I think this answers our BIG Question!
P.S. Our unique fingerprints are formed 6 months before we are even born!
BONUS BIG QUESTION: If God made and designed everyone, why did He make some people with illness?
MATCH IT!
IT'S AGAINST THE CLOCK... Get your leader to time you! 1 MIN.
TICK TICK
What did God make, when?
DAY 1 LAND, PLANTS AND TREES
DAY 2 GOD RESTED
DAY 3 ANIMALS AND PEOPLE
DAY 4 FISH AND BIRDS
DAY 5 LIGHT AND DARK
DAY 6 SUN, MOON AND STARS
DAY 7 SKY AND OCEANS
What does it mean?
WONDERSTRUCK
So where do the dinosaurs fit?
What about evolution?
SOME CRAZY BODY FACTS
(most of which science can't explain... but I can... they're things God designed JUST FOR FUN!!)
1. We produce more earwax when we're scared!
2. Human bones are stronger than concrete
3. In our lifetime we produce enough SPIT to fill 2 whole swimming pools!
4. The average adult produces 1 pint of sweat everyday from their feet!
SO... #2
Did God make me?
Why can't we make mud things come to life?
EEEW!
Psst... The world's longest ear hair was 18.1cm long. YUK!
PRAY...
Thank God for making you and designing you to be just the way you are!
AMEN!
'I am wonderstruck by the wonder of it all'

BIG Question #3

WHAT IS WORSHIP?

The Song:

WHAT A WONDERFUL WORLD

You will need:

- Paper
- Templates for making paper aeroplanes (there are loads online)
- Pens

6 mins

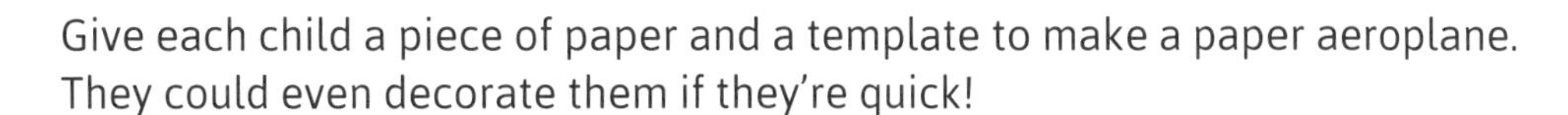

Give each child a piece of paper and a template to make a paper aeroplane. They could even decorate them if they're quick!

You will need:

- Some masking tape
- The aeroplanes the children have just made

5 mins

Create a target on the floor, with three squares inside one another. Each square is worth a different amount of points.

Get the children to throw their aeroplanes and see how many points they can get!

You will need:

- A big piece of paper
- Pens

4 mins

Set the scene:

Tell the children that the BIG Question we're thinking about today is:
What is worship?

Ask the children what they think worship is and write down their ideas on the big piece of paper - stick this up somewhere.

Tell the children that we're going be thinking about worship in more detail.

You will need:

- Story script (starting on *page 21*)

10 mins

Teach the children the trigger words and encourage them to interact as you tell them the story.

You will need:

- *Welcome to the BIG Academy* album and facilities to play it.

5 mins

Sing *What a Wonderful World* together (Track 4).

10-13 mins

You will need:

- An activity sheet copied for each child
- Pens/pencils
- Bibles

Go through the sheet - use it as a foundation for discussion. Allow the children to do the sheet however they would like to, but talk to them about the key questions as they are doing things.

5 mins

You will need:

- Lots of the same size boxes (wrapped in plain paper if you wish)
- Pens
- Sticky tape
- *Welcome to the BIG Academy* album and facilities to play it.

Give each child a box and invite them to write or draw their expression of worship on it. Play *What A Wonderful World* again as they do this.

They could write prayers of worship or draw a picture of something they think is wonderful that God has made, or perhaps even draw themselves doing something to worship God (an activity that might not 'normally' be classed as worship).

Use the boxes to build a 'worship wall'.

So... what is worship?
Showing God that we think He is wonderful.

OUTSIDE THE TEMPLE GATES (ACTS 3:1-10)

TRIGGER WORDS **Stand**, **walk**, **hop**, **skip**, **jump**: Do each action as it is read
Sitting on a mat: Everyone is to sit down
Beautiful: Do a pose as if you were having your photo taken and say, "Gorgeous darling!"

There was once a man who, from the very day he had been born, could not move his legs. He had never been able to **stand**, **walk**, **hop**, **skip** or **jump**. He would just stay **sitting on a mat**, on the floor - that is, of course, unless someone carried him elsewhere, which very often, they did. Every day, this man was carried to the temple gates, which were called **Beautiful**, where he would sit and beg for money from every passer-by.

"Money... Sir! Madam! Please? ... Help me out. Spare a few coins would you?"

Now and again people would drop a few coins in his pot. And now and again people would stare straight ahead, avoiding any eye contact, walking faster as they approached the man who could not **stand**, **walk**, **hop**, **skip** or **jump**; the man who would just remain **sitting on a mat** on the floor; they would walk straight past him and into the temple. This would happen day in, day out.

Now, today was a day just like any other. The man was carried to his usual spot - just outside the temple, next to the gates, which were called **Beautiful**. There, he sat and begged for money from every passer-by. But, on this particular day, everything was going to change for the man who could not **stand**, **walk**, **hop**, **skip** or **jump**; the man who would just remain **sitting on a mat** on the floor.

Two men, Peter and John, were on their way to the temple. These two men, Peter and John, were followers of Jesus. They were on their way to the temple for their time of prayer. As the two men approached the temple, the man who was sat outside the temple gates - the gates, which were called **Beautiful** - spotted them, and held out his hands, looking up at them as they neared.

"Money!" said the man, sat on the floor. "Money? Kind gentlemen... please... help me out. Spare a few coins would you!?"

Peter and John looked at the man as they gradually neared where he was sat, begging.

"Money!" said the man, once again. "Money? Kind gentlemen... please... help me out. Spare a few coins would you!?"

Peter and John stopped. They looked at the man - the man who could not **stand**, **walk**, **hop**, **skip** or **jump**; the man who would just remain **sitting on a mat** on the floor.

"Look at us." said Peter.

The man suddenly perked up a little. He sat up as straight as he could, held out his hands, looked Peter straight in the eyes and waited expecting to get a nice, large amount of money, enough money to see him through the next week, or month perhaps.

"This is it. Today is going to be a good day!" he thought to himself.

And today was going to be a good day, but not for the reasons that the man thought.

"Listen," said Peter. "I haven't got any silver or gold but I'll give you that which I do have! In the name of Jesus Christ, get up and walk!"

Peter then grasped the right hand of the man - the man who could not **stand**, **walk**, **hop**, **skip** or **jump**; the man who would just remain **sitting on a mat** on the floor outside the gates, which were called **Beautiful**. He grasped his hand, helped him up to his feet and instantly the man's feet, ankles and legs became strong! As strong as if he'd been using them his entire life!

"This is amazing!" said the man. "Thank you, God! Praise God! WOOO-HOOO! I can **stand**! I can **hop**! I can **skip**! And, I can **jump**! I don't have to spend another day **sitting on a mat** on the floor."

The man could not contain his excitement and joy! He ran around screaming praises to God and thanking Him at the top of his lungs. The people who saw this were absolutely amazed. They could barely believe that this was the same man who would sit outside the gates, which were called **Beautiful**. Many of the people could do nothing else but join in with the man in praising and thanking God for what had happened.

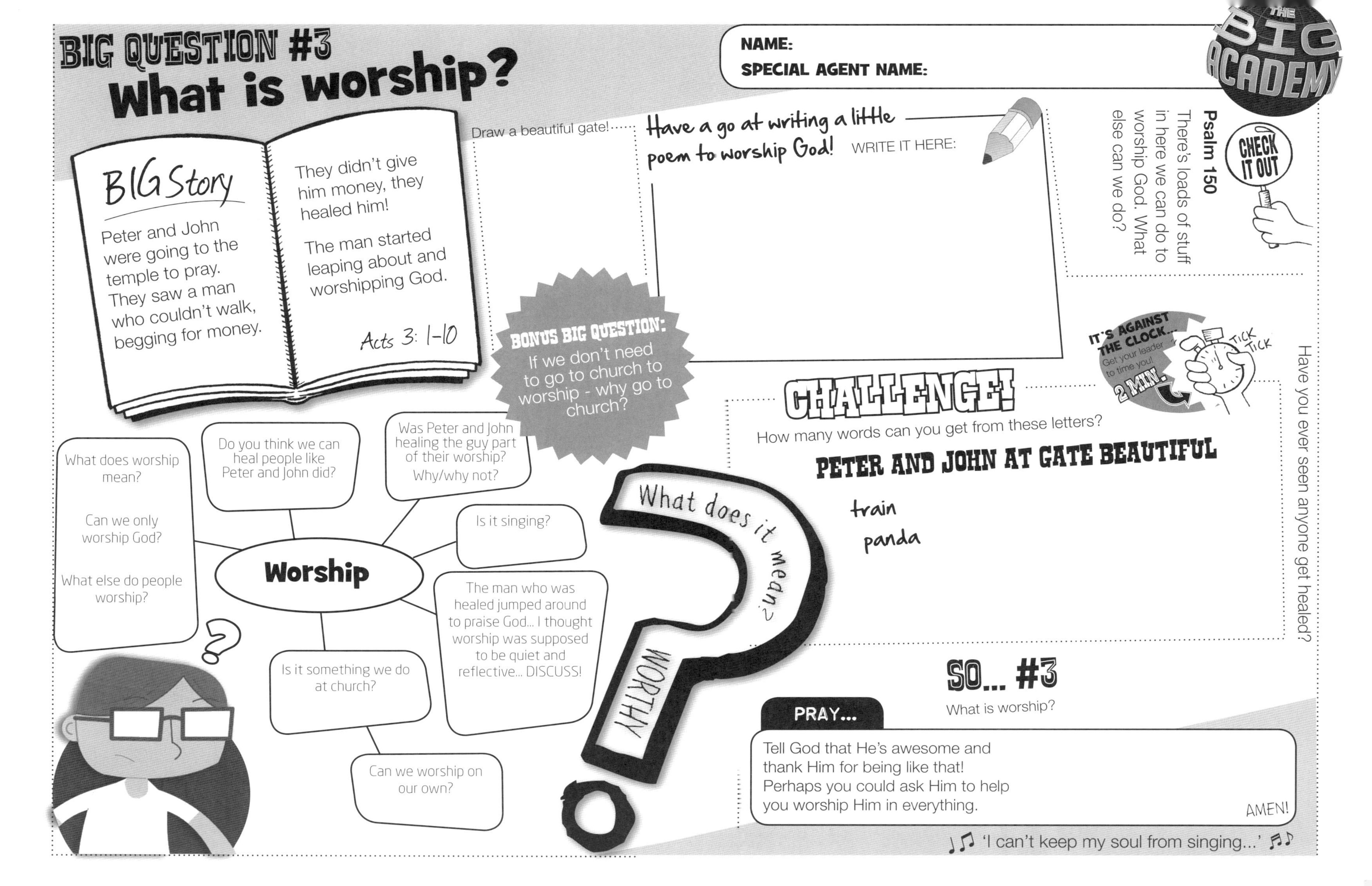

BIG QUESTION #3
What is worship?

NAME:
SPECIAL AGENT NAME:

BIG Story

Peter and John were going to the temple to pray. They saw a man who couldn't walk, begging for money.

They didn't give him money, they healed him!

The man started leaping about and worshipping God.

Acts 3: 1-10

Draw a beautiful gate!

Have a go at writing a little poem to worship God! WRITE IT HERE:

Psalm 150

There's loads of stuff in here we can do to worship God. What else can we do?

BONUS BIG QUESTION: If we don't need to go to church to worship - why go to church?

IT'S AGAINST THE CLOCK... Get your leader to time you!

CHALLENGE!

How many words can you get from these letters?

PETER AND JOHN AT GATE BEAUTIFUL

train
panda

Have you ever seen anyone get healed?

Worship

- What does worship mean?
- Can we only worship God?
- What else do people worship?
- Do you think we can heal people like Peter and John did?
- Was Peter and John healing the guy part of their worship? Why/why not?
- Is it singing?
- The man who was healed jumped around to praise God... I thought worship was supposed to be quiet and reflective... DISCUSS!
- Is it something we do at church?
- Can we worship on our own?

SO... #3

What is worship?

PRAY...

Tell God that He's awesome and thank Him for being like that!
Perhaps you could ask Him to help you worship Him in everything.

AMEN!

♩♫ 'I can't keep my soul from singing...' ♫♪

BIG Question #4

WHAT IS SIN?

The Song:

WALK WITH YOU

6 mins

You will need:

- Nothing except a bit of space!

Pick one child to be 'it' and divide the rest of the players into pairs.

Tell all the pairs to hold hands and keep holding hands throughout the game.

Give the pairs 10 seconds to run away from 'it'.

'It' then chases the pairs, trying to tag them.

If just one partner gets tagged, that eliminates the pair from the game.

If the pairs separate, that also eliminates them from the game.

The last remaining pair wins!

3 mins

You will need:

- Some pieces of paper
- Pens

Set the scene:

Give every child a piece of paper and tell them to draw something that they love.

Give them one minute to do this (they'll need to do speed-drawing!).

Then instruct them to screw it up into a ball as tight as they can. When they've done that they need to try and flatten it again!

Tell the children that the BIG Question we're thinking about today is: *What is sin?*

The piece of paper can never be the same again. Talk to the children about the fact that, now sin is in the world, our world can never be the same again - it is not how God intended it to be.

So, what on earth is sin?!

10 mins

You will need:

- Story script (starting on *page 26*)
- Three big cards - Large cardboard with A, B and C written on them.

Stick the three letters up around the room (alternatively, give them to three leaders if you have them, then they can move around!).

Throughout the story there are options to give the children with three answers to choose from - A, B and C. Get the children to run to the letter that they think gives the correct answer.

5 mins

You will need:

- *Welcome to the BIG Academy* album and facilities to play it.

Sing *Walk With You* together (Track 5).

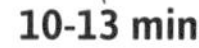

10-13 mins

You will need:

- An activity sheet copied for each child
- Pens/pencils
- Bibles

Go through the sheet - use it as a foundation for discussion. Allow the children to do the sheet however they would like to, but talk to them about the key questions as they are doing things.

8 mins

(Optional) **You will need:**

- To have a look at this site: www.freekidscrafts.com/beaded_snake-e1495.html
- Collect all relevant materials from the website

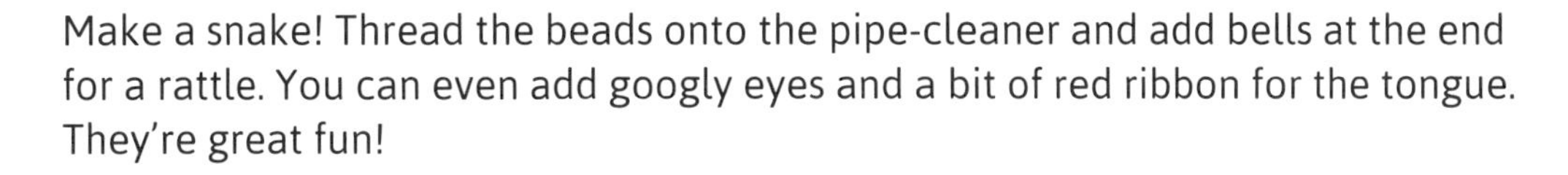

Make a snake! Thread the beads onto the pipe-cleaner and add bells at the end for a rattle. You can even add googly eyes and a bit of red ribbon for the tongue. They're great fun!

4 mins

Have a prayer time with the children.

This could be a time where they can say sorry to God for anything they've done that isn't 'walking with Him'.

You could get them to write them on pieces of paper, and then throw them all away as a symbol of God getting rid of sin.

Tell the children that God forgives them!

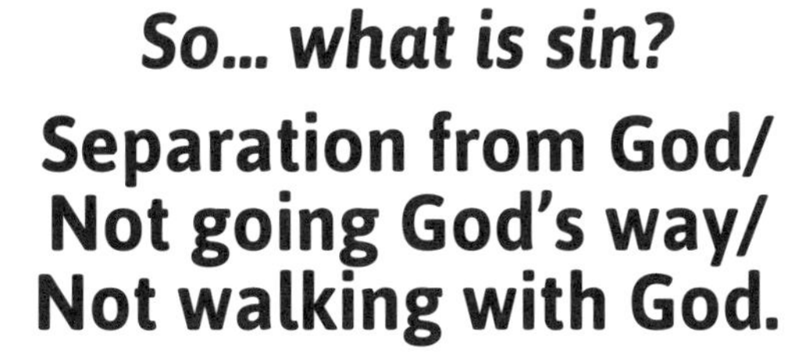

So... what is sin?

Separation from God/
Not going God's way/
Not walking with God.

THE FALL (GENESIS 3)

So, we already know the story of creation. We've heard of how God spoke and the world and everything in it came into existence... But what about the first people on earth. What's their story? Who were they?

Well, the first people that God created were a man and a woman named...

A) Alan & Eve
B) Adam & Eve
C) Burt & Janice

The first people that God created were, of course, **B**, **Adam and Eve**.

The earth was a beautiful place. God had created it and He was pleased with it. It was good. Now, there was a place where God had put Adam and Eve for them to live. A place where they could walk with Him and where they could take care of the plants and trees and animals. A place they could call their home.

But what name was given to this place? Was it called...

A) The Garden of Eden
B) The Palace of Pudding
C) The Garden of Good and Evil

The correct answer is, **A**, **The Garden of Eden**.

God placed Adam and Eve in the Garden of Eden and they lived there and walked and talked with God in the garden. It was perfect.

There were so many different plants and trees of all different shapes and sizes in the Garden of Eden. Trees that grew the most amazing ripe, plump fruit and plants that sprouted vegetables of all kinds. There was so much food - so much choice!

Adam and Eve were told that they could eat from any of the trees and plants in the garden. But, there was one tree that God told them that they must stay away from... only one that He said they must not eat from, or they would die.

But what was this tree called? Was it called...

A) The Tree of the Knowledge of Good and Evil.
B) The Good Tree of the Knowledge of Evil.
C) The Tree of Giant Chocolate Bars and Sweets.

The correct answer is, **A**, **The Tree of the Knowledge of Good and Evil**.

This was the only tree that Adam and Eve were not to eat from. So, Adam and Eve and the Lord God continued to walk and talk with one another in the Garden of Eden. It was perfect. Oh, and did I mention, Adam and Eve were naked at this point. They walked around naked all day long. But, they were not ashamed. This was normal back then at the beginning of time.

One day, a crafty, slithering snake slipped and glided its way to Eve, who was minding her own business, hanging out in the Garden of Eden. The crafty, slithering snake then spoke to Eve.

But, what did the crafty, slithering snake say to Eve?

A) Did you see that TV game show that I was on? I was in the jungle with Ant & Dec! I'M FAMOUS!
B) You won't really die if you eat from the tree of the knowledge of good and evil.
C) You really should not eat from The Tree of the Knowledge of Good and Evil.

The correct answer is, **B**, **The snake said to Eve that she wouldn't really die if she ate from The Tree of the Knowledge of Good and Evil.**

Eve then looked at the tree. Her mind started whirring.

"It does have a lot of fruit on it." she thought. "And it does look very scrumptious. And if it gives me knowledge and makes me wise then that can't be a bad thing... can it?"

And so, Eve stretched out her arm and clasped her hand tightly to a piece of the fruit. She plucked it from the tree and took one huge bite! She then handed it to Adam and between them they devoured the fruit. Then, everything changed. Immediately they became ashamed because they were naked and they quickly covered themselves up.

Then Adam and Eve heard the sound of God as He was walking through the garden in the gentle breeze.

But what did Adam and Eve do?

A) They showed off their new clothes that they had made and asked God if He was able to make them some shoes to go with their outfits.
B) They immediately got down on their knees and prayed with their faces to the ground.
C) They hid because they were naked.

And the correct answer is, **C**, **they hid**.

"Where are you?" called God to the man and woman. "Where are you?"

Adam answered God.

"We hid. We hid because we are naked and we didn't want You to see us."

God then asked if they'd eaten from the tree; the tree that He had specifically told them not to eat from.

"It was Eve!" said the man. "Eve gave me some of the fruit to eat."

God then told Adam and Eve that they were no longer allowed to do something.

But what was it that they were not allowed to do?

A) They were now only allowed to eat from the tree of life.
B) They were now not allowed to eat from the tree of life.
C) They were not allowed to listen to anymore music by Jay-Z or Coldplay.

And the correct answer is, **B**, **They could no longer eat from the tree of life**.

From that day, everything changed between man and woman and their relationship with God as they were cast out from the Garden of Eden.

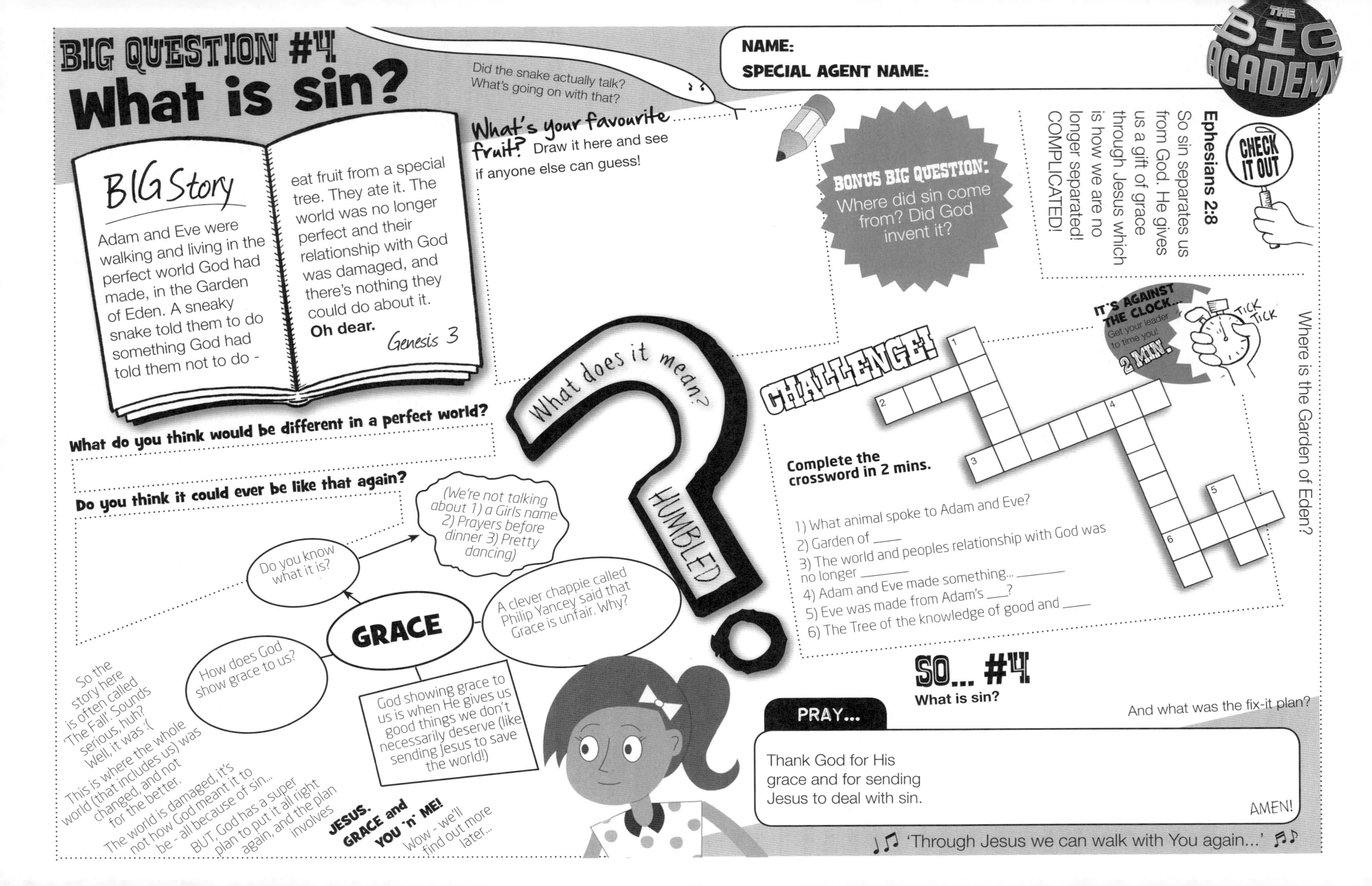

BIG QUESTION #4
What is sin?
Did the snake actually talk? What's going on with that?
NAME:
SPECIAL AGENT NAME:
THE BIG ACADEMY
BIG Story
Adam and Eve were walking and living in the perfect world God had made, in the Garden of Eden. A sneaky snake told them to do something God had told them not to do - eat fruit from a special tree. They ate it. The world was no longer perfect and their relationship with God was damaged, and there's nothing they could do about it. Oh dear.
Genesis 3
What's your favourite fruit? Draw it here and see if anyone else can guess!
BONUS BIG QUESTION: Where did sin come from? Did God invent it?
CHECK IT OUT
Ephesians 2:8
So sin separates us from God. He gives us a gift of grace through Jesus which is how we are no longer separated! COMPLICATED!
What do you think would be different in a perfect world?
Do you think it could ever be like that again?
What does it mean?
HUMBLED
CHALLENGE!
IT'S AGAINST THE CLOCK... Get your leader to time you! 2 MIN.
TICK TICK
Complete the crossword in 2 mins.
1) What animal spoke to Adam and Eve?
2) Garden of ____
3) The world and peoples relationship with God was no longer ______
4) Adam and Eve made something... ______
5) Eve was made from Adam's ___?
6) The Tree of the knowledge of good and ____
Where is the Garden of Eden?
GRACE
Do you know what it is?
(We're not talking about 1) a Girls name 2) Prayers before dinner 3) Pretty dancing)
A clever chappie called Philip Yancey said that Grace is unfair. Why?
How does God show grace to us?
God showing grace to us is when He gives us good things we don't necessarily deserve (like sending Jesus to save the world!)
So the story here is often called 'The Fall'. Sounds serious, huh? Well, it was :(
This is where the whole world (that includes us) was changed, and not for the better.
The world is damaged, it's not how God meant it to be - all because of sin...
BUT, God has a super plan to put it all right again, and the plan involves
JESUS. GRACE and YOU 'n' ME!
Wow - we'll find out more later...
SO... #4
What is sin?
And what was the fix-it plan?
PRAY...
Thank God for His grace and for sending Jesus to deal with sin.
AMEN!
'Through Jesus we can walk with You again...'

BIG Question #5

IS GOD ALWAYS FAITHFUL?

The Song:

YOU'VE BEEN FAITHFUL

5 mins

You will need:

- Building items!
  (Jenga blocks/cardboard boxes/selection of household items that will stack!)
- Lego people

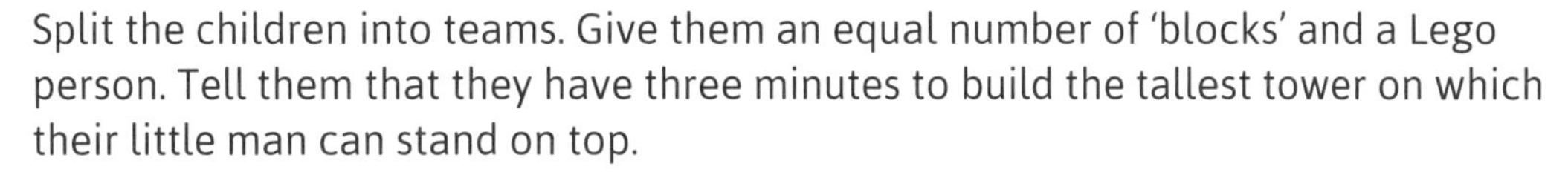

Split the children into teams. Give them an equal number of 'blocks' and a Lego person. Tell them that they have three minutes to build the tallest tower on which their little man can stand on top.

You can give the team with the tallest tower a prize... if you want to!

4 mins

You will need:

- Two leaders
- A large jigsaw (preferably with big pieces)

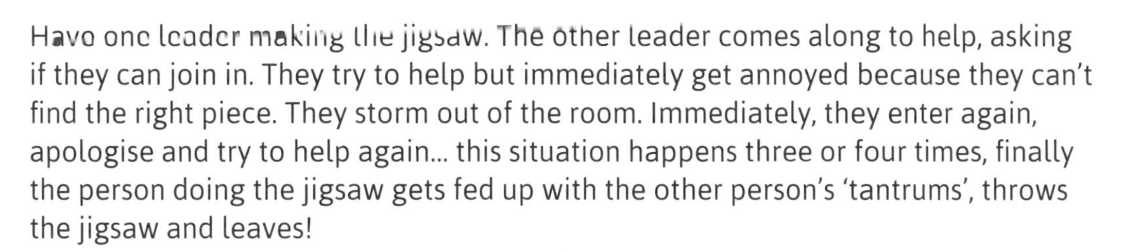

Have one leader making the jigsaw. The other leader comes along to help, asking if they can join in. They try to help but immediately get annoyed because they can't find the right piece. They storm out of the room. Immediately, they enter again, apologise and try to help again... this situation happens three or four times, finally the person doing the jigsaw gets fed up with the other person's 'tantrums', throws the jigsaw and leaves!

Set the scene:

Explain the point of your little sketch - God is NOT like that! However many times we get things wrong/say sorry/don't do things we should etc. God will never give up on us. God is faithful.

Tell the children that the BIG Question we're thinking about today is:
Is God Always Faithful?

10 mins

You will need:

- Story script (starting on *page 31*)

Teach the children the trigger words and encourage them to interact as you tell them the story.

5 mins

You will need:

- *Welcome to the BIG Academy* album and facilities to play it.

Sing *You've Been Faithful* together (Track 6).

10-13 mins

You will need:

- An activity sheet copied for each child
- Pens/pencils
- Bibles

Go through the sheet - use it as a foundation for discussion. Allow the children to do the sheet however they would like to, but talk to them about the key questions as they are doing things.

7 mins

(Optional) **You will need:**

- Brown paint
- Washing facilities
- Thin black marker pens
- Paint brushes

Make a handprint camel for each child! See picture for how to adapt the standard handprint! They can obviously add all sorts of things if you want - saddles/sand in the background/people riding on them/an extra hump... as much as your time allows!

3 mins

Ask the children this...

What difference does it make that God always has been faithful, and always will be? Does it make you want to trust Him more?

Pray with the children. Perhaps invite them to declare together, something like this:

I believe God is faithful
He will never let me down.
I believe God is faithful
I will do my best to trust Him.

FROM EGYPT TO THE PROMISED LAND (EXODUS)

TRIGGER WORDS **Hot, sandy desert**: "Hot hot hot!" and fan your face with your hand.
Promised land: "Whoopee!"
We were better off in Egypt: "Moan, moan, moan" [with a sarcastic, bad attitude, 'hand-chatting' action].

God's people, the Israelites, had been slaves in Egypt for a long time. To get them out of this mess, God decided to send a man named Moses to bring them out of the land of Egypt and into an amazing land that He had promised them.

The Israelites were excited about the **promised land**.

But, arriving at the Red Sea, the Israelites looked behind them towards Egypt, only to see hundreds of Egyptian soldiers coming after them!

Many of the Israelites felt that this was the time to have a little grumble and groan and sulk and moan.

"Oi, Moses!", said the Israelites. "Why did you bring us out of Egypt. Now we're going to die here. **We were better off in Egypt**!"

But God separated the waters of the Red Sea allowing all of the Israelites to cross over on dry land. The waters then rushed back in and the Israelites really were free from the Egyptians. Once again, the Israelites were excited about the **promised land**.

And so, Moses and the Israelites walked through the **hot, sandy desert** towards the amazing land that God had promised them.

However, many of the Israelites felt the need to have a little grumble and groan and sulk and moan.

"Oi, Moses!", said the Israelites, "we've been walking three days now and there's no sign of water anywhere! **We were better off in Egypt**."

But God provided them with water. The Israelites were, once again, excited about the **promised land**.

And so, Moses and the Israelites continued to walk through the **hot, sandy desert** towards the amazing land that God had promised them.

However, many of the Israelites felt the need to have a little grumble and groan and sulk and moan.

"Oi, Moses!", said the Israelites, "why did God bring us out of Egypt? Now we haven't got any food. We had food in Egypt, if you remember! **We were better off in Egypt**."

But, God provided them with food, and every morning they woke up to find bread outside their tents.

"We've got food! Hooray!" shouted the Israelites, forgetting what it was that they'd been grumbling about.

The Israelites were, once again, excited about the **promised land**.

And so Moses and the Israelites continued to walk through the **hot, sandy desert** towards the amazing land that God had promised them.

However, many of the Israelites felt the need to have a little grumble and groan and sulk and moan.

"Oi, Moses!", said the Israelites, "we're thirsty. Is God really with us? Because if He was, then surely we wouldn't be thirsty. **We were better off in Egypt**."

But, God told Moses to hit a rock with his staff and water would flow out from it. So Moses did just that. And just as God had said, water flowed out from the rock.

"Yey!" cheered the Israelites. "We have water!"

The Israelites were, once again, excited about the **promised land**.

And so Moses and the Israelites continued to walk through the **hot, sandy desert** towards the amazing land that God had promised them.

However, many of the Israelites felt the need to, you guessed it, have a little grumble and groan and sulk and moan.

"Oi, Moses!", said the Israelites, "this food that God keeps sending us is getting quite tiresome. We're sick of eating the same thing everyday! Tell God to send us something else! Something nice! We had nicer food in Egypt... **We were better off in Egypt**."

As you can imagine, Moses was annoyed with the Israelite people. But, still, Moses and the Israelites continued to walk through the **hot, sandy desert** towards the amazing land that God had promised them.

Unfortunately, the Israelites continued to upset God and continued to forget how good He had been to them. They continually went against what God said and continually did things which upset Him.

And so, after Moses and the Israelites had walked through the **hot, sandy desert** and eventually arrived at the amazing land that God was going to give them, they still weren't happy and they felt the need to have a little grumble and groan and sulk and moan.

"Oi, Moses", said the Israelites, "why has God brought us here? They're like giants in that land. They'll kill us. **We were better off in Egypt**."

Enough was enough! Because of their constant grumbling and groaning and sulking and moaning, and because of their disobedience, God never allowed any of the Israelites, who had once been slaves in Egypt, to enter the land that He promised them. Only their children would enter. They then wandered for 40 years in the **hot, sandy desert**.

THE BIG ACADEMY
BIG QUESTION #5
Is God always faithful?
NAME:
SPECIAL AGENT NAME:
CHECK IT OUT
Isaiah 40:29-31 and Matthew 11:28-29
Promises God makes - are they still true?
BIG Story
God freed the Israelites from Egypt where they were slaves. The Israelites kept moaning even though God was looking after them...
So, they never got to go in the promised land (but their children did!)
Exodus
Did you know?
Moses lived to 120 years old (Deuteronomy 34:7) And apparently he had great eyesight and muscles!
BONUS BIG QUESTION:
God stopped people getting into the promised land... does that mean He stopped being faithful?
How was God faithful to the Israelites?
How is God faithful to us?
How can we be faithful to God?
'You're the God of the impossible'
Hold on... does that mean God can make a stone that He can't lift? Or a square circle?
What does it mean?
PROMISE
Colour me in!
FAITHFUL
CHALLENGE!
Which path should the Israelites take to get you to the promised land? You've got 1 min!
A.
B.
C.
IT'S AGAINST THE CLOCK...
Get your leader to time you!
1 MIN.
TICK TICK
DROMISED LAND!
SO... #5
Is God always faithful?
PRAY...
Thank God that He's always faithful.
AMEN!
'Every moment throughout history, You've been good.'

BIG Question #6

HOW IS GOD WITH ME?

The Song:

STRONG AND BRAVE

6-8 mins

You will need:

- Bunch of keys
- Chairs
- Blindfold
- Junk/boxes/noisy things - include a few big items if possible.

Lay out all the junk/boxes/toys etc. in and across the middle of the room, precariously balanced - include some chairs and make it difficult to walk through. Ideally, you can't get across the room without touching things or moving things!

A child is blindfolded and sitting on a chair at one end of the room. There is a bunch of keys under their chair.

The aim is for everyone else to make their way to the person on the chair, from the opposite side of the room. Being as quiet as they can they must get the keys from under the chair. Send a few at a time.

The person who is blindfolded must be listening and point in the direction where they think someone is. If they point correctly, that person is out.

If someone gets the keys they win! If no-one does, the person on the chair wins.

4 mins

You will need:

- Copy of *Footprints in the Sand* poem
- Sand
- Tray
- Towels

Set the scene:

Get each of the children to make a footprint or two in the sand while you read them the poem.

Tell the children that the BIG Question we're thinking about today is:
How is God with me?

Ask the children how they know God is with them.

10 mins

You will need:

- Story script (starting on *page 36*)

Teach the children the trigger words and encourage them to interact as you tell them the story.

You will need:

5 mins

- *Welcome to the BIG Academy* album and facilities to play it.

Sing *Strong and Brave* together (Track 6).

TALK ABOUT IT

You will need:

10-13 mins

- An activity sheet copied for each child
- Pens/pencils
- Bibles

Go through the sheet - use it as a foundation for discussion. Allow the children to do the sheet however they would like to, but talk to them about the key questions as they are doing things.

(Optional) **You will need:**

7 mins

- Paper
- Pencils
- White fabric
- Thick cardboard
- Fabric pens

Give each child a square of fabric taped onto a piece of thick card.

Use the fabric pens to create a badge (so not too big!) that the children can have sewn into their coat/bag. Get them to come up with some sort of logo or design that will remind them that God is always with them.

NB. Make sure you send instructions for the grown-ups at home (whether or not they need to iron it to seal it, and what they are supposed to do with it).

You will need:

3-6 mins

- Finger paint
- Wet wipes
- Canvas/big piece of paper

It'd be cool to do this response on a big canvas that you could then have in your children's group room/area... but if this is stretching the budget too much, use paper!

Write these words nicely on the canvas:

We know God is with us by His Holy Spirit - We will trust Him.

Get the children to add their fingerprint to the canvas if they believe what it says!

So... how is God with me?
God is with me by His Holy Spirit.

JOSHUA (JOSHUA 1-6)

TRIGGER WORDS **River**: "Blub-blub-blub"
Trumpets: "Toot-toot"
I will never leave you: "Wooooohoooo!"
Strong and brave: Show off your muscles!

Moses had led the people of Israel out of Egypt. They were headed to the land that God had long promised them. However, before they entered the land, Moses died and a man named Joshua was chosen by God to lead His people.

"As I was with Moses", God said to Joshua, "so I will also be with you. **I will never leave you**. Do not be afraid. Be **strong and brave**."

The Israelites were camped near the Jordan **River**. They were camped on the opposite side of the **river** to the City of Jericho - the gateway to all of the land that God had promised the Israelites.

After three days of camping, Joshua made an announcement amongst the people.

"Listen up, everyone! It's time to pack up your tents and belongings. It's time to make a move. It's time to cross the Jordan **River** and take the City of Jericho."

It was a mightily big task for Joshua. He had to organise crossing the Jordan **River**, which was so deep it was almost at flooding level, I might add, and then he had to take charge of an entire city! He'd never done anything like this. But, remember what God had said to him.

"**I will never leave you**. Do not be afraid. Be **strong and brave**."

There were 1,000's of Israelites that needed to cross the deep **river**. Men, women, children, babies... No bridges, no boats. However would they cross?

The first Israelites to cross approached the **river** and then the most incredible thing happened. As soon as the first Israelite's feet touched the edge of the waters, the water stopped flowing down the **river** and gathered in a great heap leaving an empty **river** bed for everyone to cross. So, everyone was safely over the **river**.

The gates of Jericho were high and wide, strong and firm. Thick stone walls surrounded the city and armoured guards kept watch day and night. How would they get in? And once in, would the Israelites even survive against the army of Jericho?

But, remember what God had said.

"**I will never leave you**. Do not be afraid. Be **strong and brave**."

And so, Joshua led the Israelite fighting men to the City of Jericho. God told Joshua what must be done, and Joshua told the people.

"Here's what God has said we must do!" Joshua shouted as he proceeded to tell the Israelite armies exactly what they must do.

The Israelites marched around the City of Jericho once a day for six days, while seven Israelite priests blew on seven **trumpets**.

Then, on the seventh day, Joshua and the Israelites and the priests, along with their **trumpets**, marched around the City of Jericho seven times. The Israelite priests then blew on their **trumpets** and the Israelite armies shouted as loud as they could.

"RAAAAAARRR!"

The walls to the City of Jericho cracked and crumbled and tumbled and fell, smashing to the ground! The Israelites cheered.

"WOOOO-HOOOO!"

Joshua and the Israelites then charged in and took the city.

But, remember what God had said to Joshua.

"**I will never leave you**. Do not be afraid. Be **strong and brave**."

And it was true, God never did leave Joshua all the days of his life.

THE BIG ACADEMY
BIG QUESTION #6
How is God with me?
NAME:
SPECIAL AGENT NAME:
BIG Story
God chose Joshua to be a leader and told him He would never leave him on his own. Joshua was part of loads of really cool things that God helped him to do!
Joshua 1-6
Have you ever got lost?
How did you feel?
Draw something big + strong!
BONUS BIG QUESTION:
Is God with everyone?
(even those who don't like Him?!)
CHECK IT OUT
Joshua 1:5
The Bible tells us that God is with us by His Holy Spirit... What do you know about Him?
Do you think we could do some of the crazy cool stuff Joshua did?
Why/ Why not?
What does it mean?
FORSAKE
The Bible tells us that God is with us by His Holy Spirit... What do you know about Him?
Holy Spirit
Is He the same as Jesus?
Is the Holy Spirit, God? How do you know?
What does He do?
Is He scary?
Like a ghost?
What do you think about the Holy Spirit?
So, God is God, Jesus and Holy Spirit... what?
CHALLENGE!
UNSCRAMBLE THESE WORDS:
IT'S AGAINST THE CLOCK... Get your leader to time you!
2 MIN.
TICK TICK
POGWOSERO
_ _ D _ P _ _ _ _
FROEORTOM
C _ _ _ _ R _ _ _
GRNETHTS
_ T _ _ _ _ T _
SO... #6
How is God with me?
PRAY...
Thank God for promising never to leave us. Ask Him to help you know that and to be strong and brave!
AMEN!
'I can stand and face the day...'
Why did the people of Jericho die? Was God not with them?

BIG Question #7

JESUS DIED AND CAME BACK TO LIFE. HOW DOES THAT SAVE ME?

The Song:

HERO OF THE WORLD

You will need:

6-10 mins

- Gloves/hat/scarf
- Blindfold
- Really big bar of chocolate
- Knife and fork
- Two unbreakable bowls
- Straws
- Chocolate buttons
- Large dice

Now, I know it's nothing new, but it's such a great game and we've added a slight variation, adding in another number and activity.

- Throw a six - put all the clothes on and eat the chocolate with the knife and fork
- Throw a two - put a blindfold on and try to transfer the chocolate buttons from one bowl to the other using only a straw and the power of suction!

You will need:

4 mins

- Images of super heroes and a list of their super hero special talents! (Include some silly ones that aren't real super heroes if you want - such as, TV presenters)

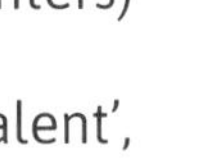

Hide the images of super heroes all around the room. Read out the 'special talent', then see who can find the correct image first.

Set the scene:

Tell the children that we're thinking about Jesus being a hero today.
The song is *Hero of the World...*

Ask the children what they think Jesus' 'special talent/power' was.

Tell the children that the BIG Question we're thinking about today is:
Jesus died and came back to life. How does that save me?

You will need:

5 mins

- *Welcome to the BIG Academy* album and facilities to play it.

Sing *Hero of the World* together (Track 7).

10 mins

You will need:

- Story script (starting on *page 41*)

You could create some images (or find some online) of Jesus doing the things mentioned in the poem, or you could just read it. If you are just reading it, make sure you're well rehearsed so that it's really engaging for the children to listen to.

10-13 mins

You will need:

- An activity sheet copied for each child
- Pens/pencils
- Bibles

Go through the sheet - use it as a foundation for discussion. Allow the children to do the sheet however they would like to, but talk to them about the key questions as they are doing things.

5-7 mins

(Optional) **You will need:**

- Sheets of 'Funky Foam' (available in most craft shops)
- Elastic
- Scissors
- Sticky foam shapes

Create superhero masks. Make a template 'mask shape' for each child, use a skewer to make holes in for the elastic. Add the elastic before you hand them out!

Give each child a mask to decorate. Provide lots of sticky foam shapes.

4-6 mins

This response is over to you!

We think this might be a perfect opportunity to ask the children if they want to follow Jesus. The best way to do this is however you think will work best with your particular group. There's a few ideas here though...

Challenge them to think about whether they want a relationship with God, everyday. Ask them if they see Jesus as the one who saves them. They could write a prayer to tell God what's going on.

You could get them to think about whether they want to do this. Perhaps they could lie on the floor and listen to *I Turn to You* (on *God's Love is Unstoppable* by BIG Ministries or also available individually on iTunes).

Get some really cheap teaspoons, and get them to think of a Thank you, Sorry, Please (tsp) prayer.

The crucial thing with this sort of response is to make sure that you give each individual child time and space to figure it out. It could be that you give them the challenge and ask them to come and talk to you next week if they want to know more.

So... Jesus died and came back to life. How does that save me?

For centuries people have been trying to answer this question. To be honest, we don't really know how it works, but we believe it does!

JESUS - LIFE, DEATH, RESURRECTION (THE GOSPELS)

Of course, I know, you've heard it before
The story of Bethlehem and of a baby born

The story of Jesus, born into this world
Born for a reason, God's plan would unfurl

Wise men, shepherds and angels did come
Bringing praise to the King, to the Holy One

But, remaining a baby was not part of this story
More was to happen, for which all would give glory

To help and to heal, to teach and to save
A way in this world, His life, it would pave

But what was to happen and who ever knew?
And what does this mean, for me and for you?

Of course, I know, you've heard it before
Jesus healed the blind, the sick and the poor

He showed others kindness, gave the time that He had
He transformed sad hearts into those that were glad

And recalling that time - the disciples in fear
But at Jesus' words, the storm it did clear

Eating food at the house of greedy Zacchaeus
But Zacchaeus did change after chatting with Jesus

Those who were lonely, and those in despair
Jesus showed love, compassion and care

But what was to happen and who ever knew?
And what does this mean, for me and for you?

Of course, I know, you've heard it before
Jesus was arrested, and knocked to the floor

He was beat up and bruised, spat on and hurt
He was kicked and ill-treated and left in the dirt

He was nailed up high, nailed high to a cross
He was nailed up high, His life would be lost

Some mocked, some jeered, some laughed at His pain
Some watched, some cried, while others would pray

With a last gasp, a last breath, Jesus was dead
The spear in his side, crown of thorns on His head

But what was to happen and who ever knew?
And what does this mean, for me and for you?

Of course, I know, you've heard it before
It does not end here, for this story has more

The third day of His death, with the stone rolled away
In the tomb that was guarded, no body did lay

Was Jesus gone? Was He taken away?
No! He's alive! He is alive once again!

He appeared to the disciples and many He knew
Jesus had risen! He's alive! It was true!

Living and breathing, nail-marked hands and feet
He's living today and one day we shall meet

So that is what happened and who ever knew?
But what does this mean, for me and for you?

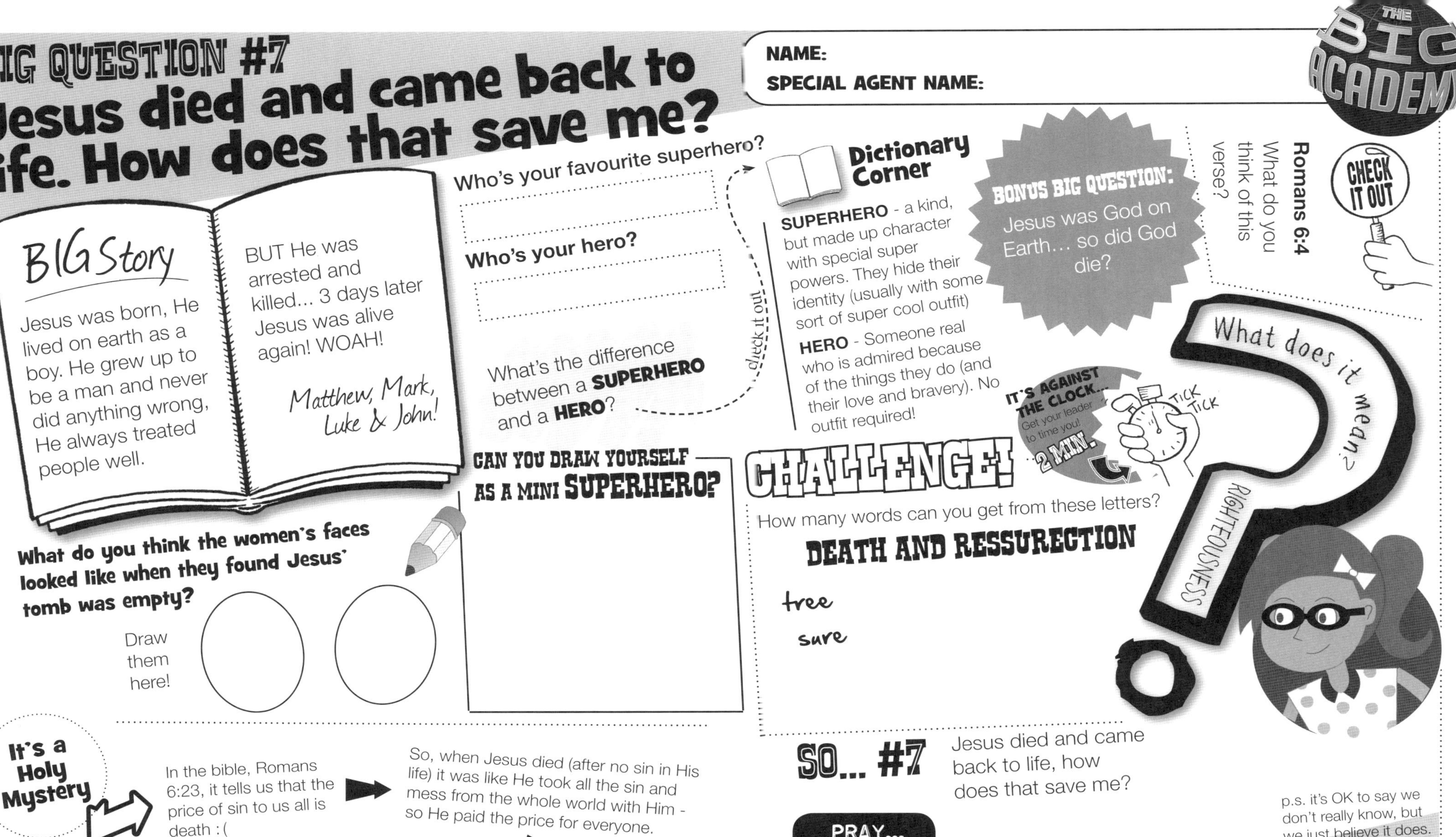

BIG QUESTION #7
Jesus died and came back to life. How does that save me?

NAME:

SPECIAL AGENT NAME:

THE BIG ACADEMY

BIG Story

Jesus was born, He lived on earth as a boy. He grew up to be a man and never did anything wrong, He always treated people well.

BUT He was arrested and killed... 3 days later Jesus was alive again! WOAH!

Matthew, Mark, Luke & John!

Who's your favourite superhero?

Who's your hero?

What's the difference between a **SUPERHERO** and a **HERO**?

check it out

Dictionary Corner

SUPERHERO - a kind, but made up character with special super powers. They hide their identity (usually with some sort of super cool outfit)

HERO - Someone real who is admired because of the things they do (and their love and bravery). No outfit required!

BONUS BIG QUESTION: Jesus was God on Earth... so did God die?

CHECK IT OUT

Romans 6:4

What do you think of this verse?

What does it mean?

RIGHTEOUSNESS

What do you think the women's faces looked like when they found Jesus' tomb was empty?

Draw them here!

CAN YOU DRAW YOURSELF AS A MINI SUPERHERO?

CHALLENGE!

IT'S AGAINST THE CLOCK... Get your leader to time you! 2 MIN.

TICK TICK

How many words can you get from these letters?

DEATH AND RESSURECTION

tree

sure

It's a Holy Mystery

In the bible, Romans 6:23, it tells us that the price of sin to us all is death : (

So, when Jesus died (after no sin in His life) it was like He took all the sin and mess from the whole world with Him - so He paid the price for everyone.

Jesus coming back to life and beating death (woo-hoo) was the start of God's super-fix-it plan for the world. (It was as if Jesus left all the mess behind in the grave when He came back to life.)

To be honest, it is a complete mystery how this actually works, and people with mega brains have been trying to explain it for hundreds of years (and not really succeeding!). All we know is that somehow what Jesus did gives us the opportunity to live with God (just like we were meant to), and also to do that forever!

SO... #7

Jesus died and came back to life, how does that save me?

p.s. it's OK to say we don't really know, but we just believe it does.

PRAY...

Thank Jesus for what He did to save the world (and you!)

AMEN!

♩♫ 'There is no greater hero...Jesus the Hero of the World' ♬♪

If Jesus has beaten death, then why do we still die?

BIG Question #8

WHAT DOES IT MEAN TO TRUST JESUS?

The Song:

YESTERDAY, TODAY, FOREVER

5-7 mins

You will need:

- Scarves/strips of material
- Some space!
- Cones/tape to mark the floor

Organise your children into pairs (making sure they're of similar height) and have a three-legged race - you can do this however you think would work best for your group.

3 mins

You will need:

- Two presents wrapped up:
  1. Very pretty and neat and exciting-looking with something not very good inside (perhaps a packet of dates or something?).
  2. Make it not look like a present - use newspaper, make it really tatty and covered in dirt and rips. But put something really exciting inside - perhaps a massive bag of sweets!

Give the children the option of choosing one item or the other. Let them choose!

(Bear in mind with older children they'll probably guess what you're doing, but the illustration still works!) In theory they'll choose the nice looking item. Tell them that the tatty thing is actually better... will they trust you?

Set the scene:

Tell the children that the BIG Question we're thinking about today is:
What does it mean to trust Jesus?

Sometimes trusting Jesus doesn't seem like the most appealing thing to do, but it is always the best thing to do.

10 mins

You will need:

- Story script (starting on *page 46*)
- Dressing-up clothes (an outfit for Ananias)

The story is a monologue, Ananias' account of the transformation of Saul.

Make sure you've read the story through a few times so you can read it with feeling! Dress up as Ananias and go for it! (I imagine you walking around a bit, being quite animated as you tell the story!)

5 mins

You will need:

- *Welcome to the BIG Academy* album and facilities to play it.

Sing *Yesterday, Today, Forever* together (Track 8).

You will need:

- An activity sheet copied for each child
- Pens/pencils
- Bibles

Go through the sheet - use it as a foundation for discussion. Allow the children to do the sheet however they would like to, but talk to them about the key questions as they are doing things.

(Optional) **You will need:**

- Rich tea biscuits (or fairy cakes if you have time to make them)
- Thick water icing in a few colours
- Sprinkles/sweets
- Writing icing

Give each child a few biscuits/cakes to decorate.

They could write 'Trust Jesus' on their biscuits, and then could give them away to someone.

Or, you could just have fun decorating biscuits!

You will need:

- Nice round stones, nice sizes to hold
- Permanent markers (or paint if you're feeling brave!)
- Squares of card (big enough for the stones to sit on)
- Felt tips

Give a stone to each of the children and help them write 'Jesus never changes' on the stone. They could colour it a bit if they want. Then get them to write 'I will trust Him' on the card, and decorate it. So if they lift the stone, they can see 'I will trust Him' underneath.

With smaller children, you could have the stones ready prepared. You could even print onto the squares 'I will trust Him', ready for them to colour in.

Tell the children to put their stone somewhere they'll see it, to remind them to trust Jesus, and that He never changes, and He'll help us do whatever He asks us to do.

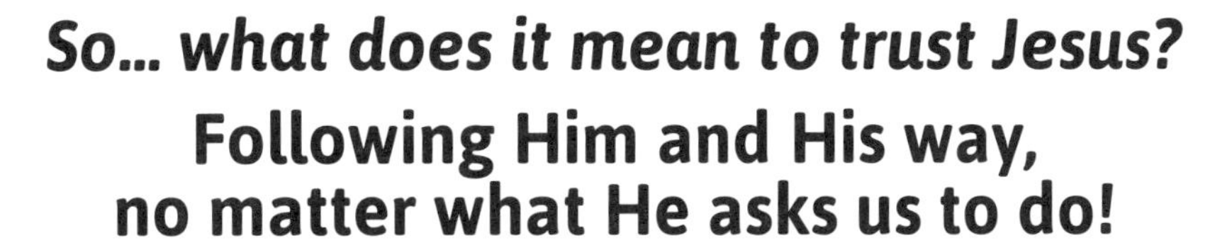

ANANIAS VISITS SAUL (ACTS 9)

I am exhausted! What a day I've had! I'm Ananias. I live in the City of Damascus - don't worry, I don't expect you to have heard of me. However, I do expect you to do one thing - listen to my story! It's a good one. I've never been so scared, but I knew I had to trust Jesus.

Have you ever had to go and meet someone that you really didn't want to meet? - I mean, really didn't want to meet! A little bit like when you've been in trouble at school and have been called to the headmaster's office, or perhaps your Mum or Dad have called you down from your bedroom and you just know that you've done something wrong! Remember that nervous feeling that you get where your stomach goes all funny... well, what happened to me today made me feel a little bit like that - and I say, 'a little bit like that' because actually this made me feel 100 times worse.

Last night I was chilling out, relaxing, when all of a sudden I had a vision and Jesus—that's right, Jesus!—spoke to me; Me! Ananias! And you'll never guess what He told me. It wasn't, "Ananias I have something very exciting for you", or, "Ananias, I'm sending you to the Bahamas" - No, it was nothing like that. It was, "Ananias, go and see a man called Saul. He's staying in a house on Straight Street and he's blind. Place your hands on him and he'll be able to see again."

You may not think that sounds too bad. I mean, making a blind person see is surely a good thing... right? But the thing that you must understand is that this man, Saul, was no ordinary man. He was on his way to Damascus to arrest Christians! To arrest people just like ME! He would throw Christians in jail and would quite happily have them killed. It was while he was on his way to Damascus that Saul was stopped in his tracks by a blinding light. The same blinding light that, well, left him blind. It was Jesus! Jesus spoke to him. However, I didn't know this at the time. You understand why I was scared now?

Anyway, Jesus spoke to me through this vision and, as I'm sure you can imagine, I didn't want to go. Then Jesus told me that I must go because Saul had been chosen to spread the good news about Him. I couldn't quite believe it... would you?! But, then I thought to myself, it's not everyday that one has a vision of Jesus and receives a direct instruction from Him, so I had to just trust Jesus. So with that, I was off; off to Straight Street; off to visit Saul.

Arriving at the house on Straight Street, I asked for Saul and was then taken to a room where I found him kneeling and praying. Apparently he'd been doing this for three days and hadn't had anyhing to eat or drink! Placing my hands on Saul, immediately he could see! I think I was more amazed than he was. He was baptised, ate some food and was completely transformed from who he was before. No longer did he hate Christians, or Jesus for that matter. Now, he was a Christian, and he loved Jesus! He even wants to come and meet more Christians... and not to arrest them! And, he's excited about doing some teaching in the synagogues!

I can't wait to see what Jesus has in store for Saul! Where's Jesus going to send him? What exactly is Saul going to do for Jesus? It's so exciting! I'm so happy to have been part of it. I'm so happy that I trusted Jesus and didn't ignore what He told me to do.

Well, that's all from me for now. Thanks so much for listening. Perhaps you have a story to tell about trusting Jesus?

BIG QUESTION #8
What does it mean to trust Jesus?
NAME:
SPECIAL AGENT NAME:
THE BIG ACADEMY
BIG Story
Jesus told Ananias to go and visit Saul (a Christian killer)...
He went and Saul had changed!
He then became someone who told others about Jesus!
Acts 9
Ever done anything really scary?
On your own?
Has Jesus ever spoken to you?
How?
BONUS BIG QUESTION:
How can we trust Jesus? We can't see Him!
CHECK IT OUT
Matt 16:24-25
'take up your cross'?
- What's that?
What does it mean?
UNCHANGING
What do you do in a normal day? (Draw a cartoon strip)
Does God get old?
Jesus is with you in all of these things - How does that make you feel?
Is there anything you can think of that has been the same forever and will always be?
CHALLENGE!
Ananias really had to trust Jesus - but he knew Jesus had spoken to him + would be with him.
Find 7 of the zillion ways God speaks...
IT'S AGAINST THE CLOCK...
Get your leader to time you!
2 MIN.
TICK TICK
L S A M Z E Y F N M G U
O D M V X S Y X Z K Q J
U N I M M J N Y R B A Y
D E K A S G N I L E E F
X I E Q B J N R L V O Q
U R O G T H O U G H T S
D F Y P U N B I B L E K
bible
dreams
friends
loud
thoughts
feelings
SO... #8
What does it mean to trust Jesus?
PRAY...
Why not ask God to speak to you...
...(Now try doing what He says!)
AMEN!
'Yesterday, today, forever, Jesus I can count on You.'

BIG Question #9

HOW CAN WE LIVE LIKE JESUS?

The Song:

THE WAY THAT YOU SEE

6 mins

You will need:

- A box with a hand-sized hole cut in one side of it, and an open side the other.
- Some material to cover the box
- A selection of items - food, plants, toys etc. Some messy, some not!
- Wet wipes/towel

Without showing anyone the items, place them one at a time into the box through the open side. Get the children to put their hand inside the box, through the hole that you've cut, to see if they can guess what the item is.

3 mins

You will need:

- A kaleidoscope
- An everyday object (perhaps a toaster!)

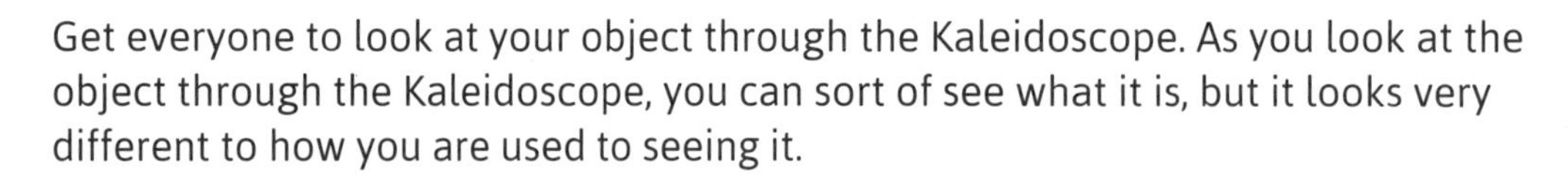

Get everyone to look at your object through the Kaleidoscope. As you look at the object through the Kaleidoscope, you can sort of see what it is, but it looks very different to how you are used to seeing it.

Set the scene:

Tell the children that we can begin to live like Jesus if we try to see things as God sees them. God sees everything we do, but often He sees it differently.

Tell the children that the BIG Question we're thinking about today is:
How can we live like Jesus?

10 mins

You will need:

- Story script (starting on *page 50*)

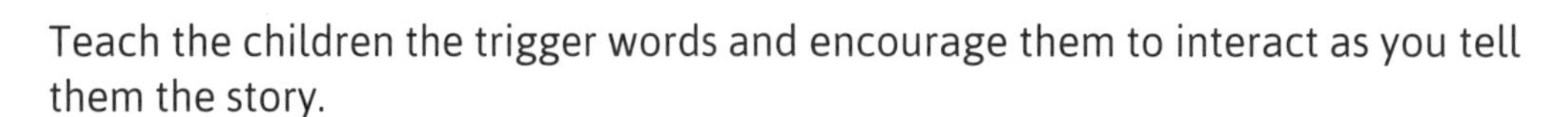

Teach the children the trigger words and encourage them to interact as you tell them the story.

5 mins

You will need:

- *Welcome to the BIG Academy* album and facilities to play it.

Sing *The Way That You See* together (Track 9).

You will need:

10-12 mins

- An activity sheet copied for each child
- Pens/pencils
- Bibles

Go through the sheet - use it as a foundation for discussion. Allow the children to do the sheet however they would like to, but talk to them about the key questions as they are doing things.

(Optional) **You will need:**

7-10 mins

- PVA glue and spreaders
- Sand (coloured or sparkly sand if you can get it)
- Black paper

Do some sand art with the children. Get them to draw a picture with the glue, and then sprinkle the sand over to create the picture. You may need to leave them to dry for a few days (depending on how restrained they are with the glue!).

You will need:

4 mins

- Pipe cleaners

Invite everyone to make a pair of glasses out of a couple of pipe cleaners as a reminder that we need to try and see things how God sees them.

So... how can we live like Jesus?

Try to see things how God sees them - and do what we think Jesus would do.

WHO WILL THROW THE FIRST STONE? (JOHN 8:1-11)

TRIGGER WORDS **Trouble**: "Dun dun duuuun!"
Crowd: Half of the children say, "Yada-yada-yada-yada", while the other half say, "Rhubarb-rhubarb-rhubarb-rhubarb" at the same time.

Many of the religious teachers did not like Jesus. In their eyes He was a problem; to them He was **trouble**. If they had their way, they would have Him arrested as soon as possible.

And so the religious teachers continued to attempt to catch Jesus out by tricking Him into doing or saying something wrong that would get Him into **trouble**.

One particular day, whilst Jesus was in the temple courts teaching a large **crowd**, some of the religious teachers approached Him.

Along with the religious teachers was a woman, being grasped tightly by each of her arms as she was dragged into the middle of the **crowd**.

She was looking very scared. She was in **trouble**.

"This woman has been caught doing something VERY wrong!" announced one of the religious teachers. "According to the laws that Moses taught in the Old Testament, we must throw stones at her until she is dead! So, Jesus, what do you think we should do with her? Should we stone her?"

Now, the religious teachers were once again trying to trick Jesus. If He said yes then He would be in **trouble** with the Roman rulers for her death. And if He said no, then He would be in **trouble** with the Jews and religious teachers.

The **crowd** of people and the religious teachers stood facing Jesus with stones clenched in the palms of their hands, each one of them ready to hurl them at the petrified woman. But Jesus didn't. He just sat there and began writing with His finger in the dusty ground.

Confused at what Jesus was doing, once again the religious teachers asked...

"So? Should we stone this woman or not?"

Jesus sat up, faced the people and said to them...

"If any one of you is without sin and has never done anything wrong then they should throw the first stone at this woman."

And with those words, Jesus then looked down and continued writing with his finger in the dusty ground. Every one of the people had done something wrong; every one of them had been in **trouble**; every single person in the **crowd**. One by one the **crowd** of people began to disburse. They walked past the woman, dropping their stones alongside her on the way. Jesus sat up again and, after looking around and seeing that it was only He and the woman left, He said to her...

"Where's everyone gone? Has no-one thrown stones at you?"

"No!" said the woman. "No-one has. They've all gone."

"Neither will I throw stones at you." Jesus replied "You can go now, but stop living life the wrong way."

And like that, the woman who was in **trouble** walked away unharmed. Hopefully she started living her life the right way from that point on.

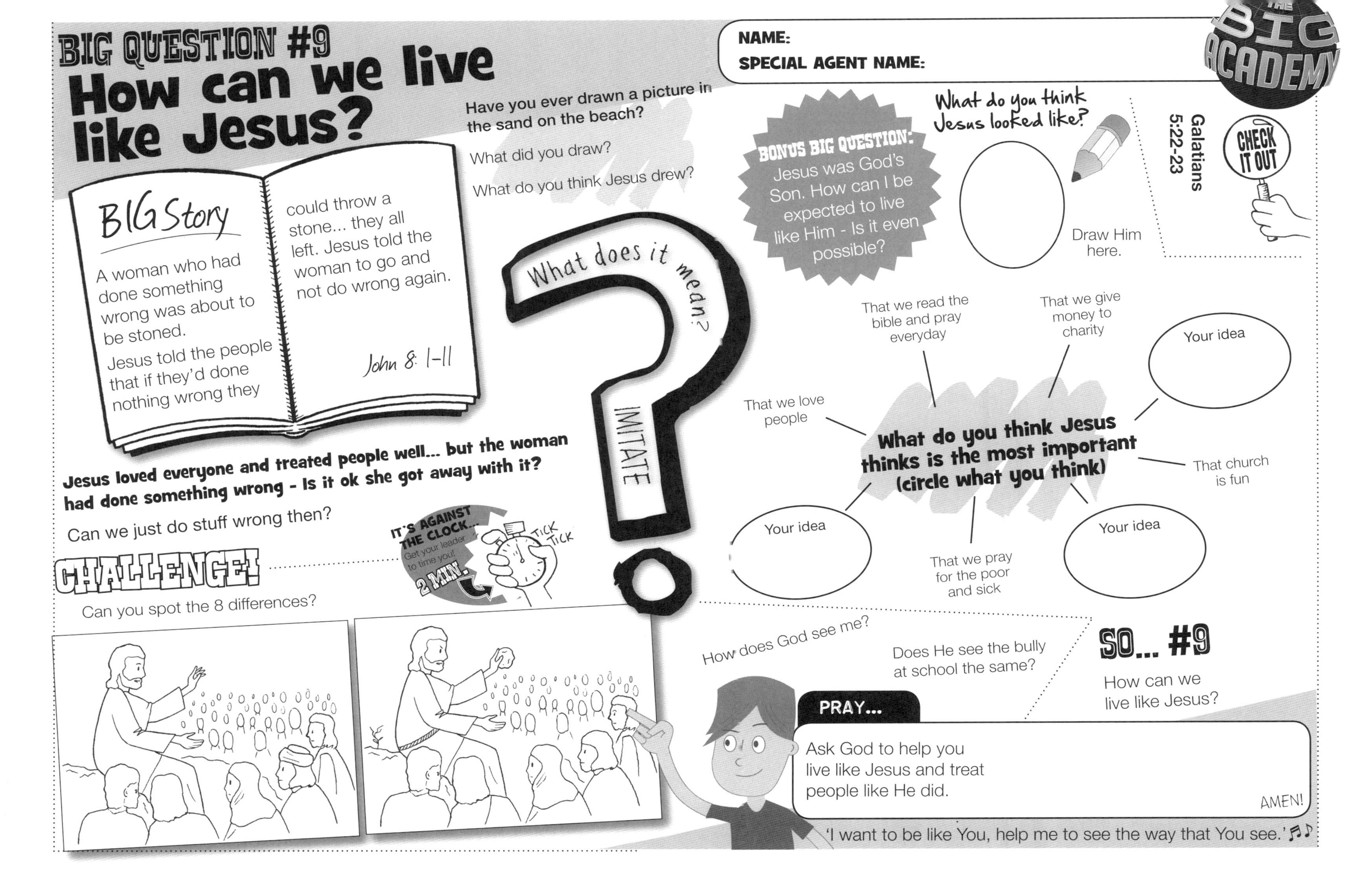
BIG QUESTION #9
How can we live like Jesus?
NAME:
SPECIAL AGENT NAME:
THE BIG ACADEMY
Have you ever drawn a picture in the sand on the beach?
What did you draw?
What do you think Jesus drew?
BIG Story
A woman who had done something wrong was about to be stoned.
Jesus told the people that if they'd done nothing wrong they could throw a stone... they all left. Jesus told the woman to go and not do wrong again.
John 8: 1-11
What does it mean?
IMITATE
Jesus loved everyone and treated people well... but the woman had done something wrong - Is it ok she got away with it?
Can we just do stuff wrong then?
CHALLENGE!
Can you spot the 8 differences?
IT'S AGAINST THE CLOCK...
Get your leader to time you!
2 MIN.
TICK TICK
BONUS BIG QUESTION:
Jesus was God's Son. How can I be expected to live like Him - Is it even possible?
What do you think Jesus looked like?
Draw Him here.
CHECK IT OUT
Galatians 5:22-23
What do you think Jesus thinks is the most important (circle what you think)
That we read the bible and pray everyday
That we give money to charity
That we love people
That church is fun
That we pray for the poor and sick
Your idea
Your idea
Your idea
How does God see me?
Does He see the bully at school the same?
SO... #9
How can we live like Jesus?
PRAY...
Ask God to help you live like Jesus and treat people like He did.
AMEN!
'I want to be like You, help me to see the way that You see.'

BIG Question #10

IS CHURCH IMPORTANT?

The Song:

SHINE LIKE STARS

5-8 mins

You will need:

- Two pieces of newspaper (per team)

Split into two teams. Starting at one end of the room, and without touching the floor, you must get your entire team to the other side of the room using only the two pieces of newspaper to stand on.

4 mins

You will need:

- Marker cones/goal posts

Set the scene:

Set up a mini-football pitch and split everyone into two teams. Get each team to stand in their goals. Tell everyone that in this game they are all goal-keepers.

Ask them what needs to happen to make the game work?

Now ask the children if they think that Church would work if everyone did the same job.

Tell the children that the BIG Question we're thinking about today is:
Is Church important?

10 mins

You will need:

- Story script (starting on *page 54*)
- Some food to share (perhaps some kind of 'tear and share' food or cakes?)

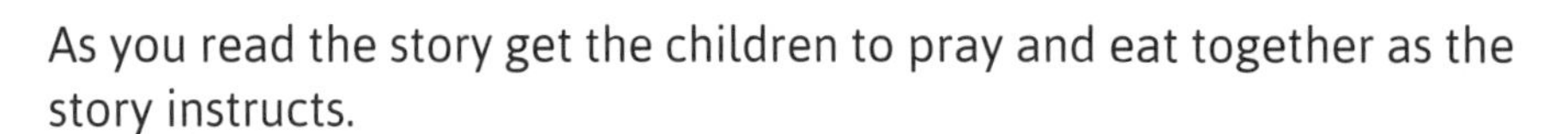

As you read the story get the children to pray and eat together as the story instructs.

5 mins

You will need:

- *Welcome to the BIG Academy* album and facilities to play it.

Sing *Shine Like Stars* together (Track 10).

10-12 mins

You will need:

- An activity sheet copied for each child
- Pens/pencils
- Bibles

Go through the sheet - use it as a foundation for discussion. Allow the children to do the sheet however they would like to, but talk to them about the key questions as they are doing things.

8-12 mins

(Optional) **You will need:**

- A load of junk (cardboard boxes, plastic bottles, coloured paper - whatever you can find)
- Sticky tape
- Scissors

With everyone working together, they must all decide what they are going to create from all of the junk. It can be anything! Next, all they need to do is make it... as a team!

4 mins

You will need:

- Tea-lights (or battery equivalent) one for everybody.

First you'll need to darken the room. Next, light on your tea-light (everyone else's tea-light should remain unlit at this point). Explain that your tea-light does make a difference, even though it's on its own - it can still be seen in the dark.

Invite everyone else to light their tea-lights (or light them for them) if they would like to be part of God's Church and if they would like to make a difference together.

With other people's tea-lights now lit, the the room will be a lot brighter. Explain that this is similar to when we work together for God, as the church. We can make much more of a difference in the world, together.

So... is Church important?

YES!

THE FIRST CHURCH (ACTS 2:42-47)

This story is about the very first church and the things that they did. One of these things was to pray. Maybe it'd be a good idea to pray before we continue with the story.

[Ask if anyone would like to pray before you continue.]

Jesus had died, He had come back to life, He had been with the disciples for 40 days and then He gave them this command before He was taken up to heaven.

"Don't leave Jerusalem, but wait here for the gift that my Father has promised you - The Holy Spirit."

At this point in time there were only about 120 Christians; 120 people who believed in Jesus. They were the first church and they would meet with one another and pray and eat food together. Maybe it'd be a good idea to eat some food together as we continue with the story.

[Hand out some food to share amongst everyone.]

For three days they waited for the Holy Spirit, who had been promised to them.

The day then came. All of the Christians were meeting together when they received the Holy Spirit. Enabled by the Holy Spirit, they began to do and say amazing things. That day, about 3,000 more people believed in Jesus and were added to the Church.

The first church, which was now a great deal bigger than 120 people, would meet together regularly. They would learn together; they would eat together; they would pray together, and together they would remember what Jesus had done for them. Not only that, but they would share their possessions with those who were in need, even if it meant selling what they had in order to give money to those who were poor. They enjoyed one another's company as they hung out together and they praised God every day for His goodness. Every day more and more people would believe in Jesus and join the church.

THE BIG ACADEMY
BIG QUESTION #10
Is Church important?
NAME:
SPECIAL AGENT NAME:
BIG Story
The first church did these things: learnt together ate together...
prayed together and remembered Jesus together.
Acts 2: 42-47
Is your church like this?
Do you eat at church?
Do you go to any clubs?
What's your favourite?
What does it mean?
FELLOWSHIP
BONUS BIG QUESTION: Is going to church the same as just hanging out with your mates?
CHECK IT OUT
1 Peter 2: 9-10
Our job as the church is to do God's work with Him + tell others! To shine like stars together. Think how much brighter a galaxy is than 1 little star
What would happen at your ideal church?
How can we shine like stars?
Should church be cutside of a building so we can 'shine'?
CHALLENGE!
IT'S AGAINST THE CLOCK... Get your leader to time you! 1 MIN.
TICK TICK
How many little people can you squeeze into this church?
SO... #10
Is Church important?
PRAY...
Ask God to help you and the rest of your church to shine like stars for Him.
AMEN!
'we will burst to light like a firework...'
Do you ever get bored in church? If so, you're not alone... read Acts 20:7-12!

BIG Question #11

HOW AM I SUPPOSED TO TELL PEOPLE ABOUT JESUS?

The Song:

READY OR NOT

5-7 mins

You will need:

- A few short phrases

Play a game of Chinese Whispers. If you have time, let the children start a few off too.

3 mins

You will need:

- Salt 'n' Shake crisps - two packets. (Add salt to only one of the packets.)
- Drinks

Give each child a couple of non-salted crisps.

Then give each child a couple of salted crisps.

Set the scene:

Tell the children that, whether they prefer the salted or unsalted, the crisps taste completely different. Salt makes a massive difference to food - you could say that it transforms it.

Tell the children that the BIG Question we're thinking about today is:
How am I supposed to tell people about Jesus?

We're going to be thinking about how we can be like salt in the world.

10 mins

You will need:

- Story script (starting on *page 58*)
- Two leaders
- Newspaper
- Bible
- Salt shaker
- Three torches - small, medium and very big/bright!

This story/sketch should be fairly engaging as it's quite silly, so no specific interaction for this one.

When you've finished the story, tell everyone that in the Bible Jesus asks us to be like salt and light in the world. Ask the children what they think that could mean? Have a little chat about it, but don't give them too many answers - that'll come in the talk about it section!

5 mins

You will need:

- *Welcome to the BIG Academy* album and facilities to play it.

Sing *Ready or Not* together (Track 11).

10-13 mins

You will need:

- An activity sheet copied for each child
- Pens/pencils
- Bibles

Go through the sheet - use it as a foundation for discussion. Allow the children to do the sheet however they would like to, but talk to them about the key questions as they are doing things.

7-10 mins

(Optional) **You will need:**

- LOTS of salt - cheapest table salt is the best
- Coloured chalk
- Babyfood jars with lids - or something of similar size (one for each child)
- Paper (A3 might be the best)
- A vacuum cleaner (and sheeting to do this activity on)

Give everyone a piece of paper, and pour salt on to it (about enough to make a good couple of centimetres depth in the jar). Then get the children to 'colour' the salt by rubbing the chalk back and forth over the salt until it's the colour they want.

Tip it into the jar using the paper as a funnel (you can create interesting effects if you tip it in at an angle).

Do as many colours as you want, or will fit, and create a 'rainbow of salt'!

NB. DON'T PICK UP the jars until full as it will all become brown and yukky then!

For images/guidance check out:
www.flaxandtwine.com/2011/03/rainbow-in-jar.html#

You could even make some little flags (using paper and cocktail sticks) to stick on the jars that say 'be like salt in the world' to help the children remember what you've been talking about.

5-10 mins

You will need:

- Glow-in-the-dark modelling clay

Create a star from the clay.

Invite everyone to write their initials on their star if they would like to 'shine' for Jesus! - To tell others about Him by the way they live and how they treat people.

If you have time you could make a few stars and create a mobile to hang from the ceiling.

So... how am I supposed to tell people about Jesus?

Not necessarily with words!
We can tell people about Jesus through the way we live.

SALT & LIGHT (BASED ON MATTHEW 5:13-16)

*[**PERSON 1** is sat reading a newspaper. **PERSON 2** is sat reading a Bible. **PERSON 2** is very confused by the Bible passage in which they're reading about salt and light and they begin licking their hands, arms and, finally, their feet in order to find out how salty they are. **PERSON 1** notices.]*

PERSON 1 Erm, I've got to ask... What are you doing? You look ridiculous!

PERSON 2 *[Whilst licking their feet or hands]* I'm just licking my feet.

PERSON 1 Yes, I can see that? But, why? You're making me feel sick! What's wrong with you?

PERSON 2 Why?! Why?! Do you not read your Bible? Matthew 5 vs 13 says this: *"Let me tell you why you are here. You're here to be salt seasoning that brings out the God-flavours of this earth. If you lose your saltiness how will people taste godliness? You've lost your usefulness and will end up in the rubbish bin!"*

Oh no! I'm going to end up in the rubbish!! I don't taste of salt!

PERSON 1 *[Attempting to explain the passage]* Hold on! You've got it wrong...

PERSON 2 *[Ignoring **Person 1**]* Quick! Find me some salt!

PERSON 1 Just listen to me a moment.

PERSON 2 Fine! I'll look for some salt myself.

*[**PERSON 2** disappears for a moment while they search for a salt shaker. Seconds later they re-appear with a salt shaker and begin shaking it all over themselves (You may want to pretend)]*

PERSON 2: I have it! I am going to be so salty, just as God wants me to be! And most certainly more salty than you!

*[**Person 2** picks up their Bible again]*

PERSON 1 But, you've got it all wrong! It doesn't mean...

PERSON 2 *[Interrupting]* Right, where was I?... Here we go... Matthew chapter 5 vs 14-15... *"You're here to be a light, bringing out the God colours in the world. God is not a secret to be kept. We're going public with this, as public as a city on a hill. If I make you light-bearers, you don't think I'm going to hide you under a bucket, do you? I'm putting you on a light stand. Now that I've put you there on a hilltop, on a light stand - shine!"*

Oh no! I'm no way near bright enough for God. Right, I need a light!

PERSON 1 This is crazy! You've got it wrong... AGAIN!

PERSON 2 We'll see who's got it wrong when I'm saltier AND brighter than you! Have you got a torch anywhere?

PERSON 1 You don't need a torch. If you listen to me I'll explain...

PERSON 2 Forget it then. I can find my own torch!

*[**PERSON 2** disappears again momentarily and re-appears with a really small torch that they shine on themselves.]*

PERSON 2 Is this bright enough do you think? Hmmm... It's not that bright really... I need something brighter... I'll just be a moment.

PERSON 1 Whatever...

*[**PERSON 2** disappears again momentarily and re-appears with a slightly larger, brighter torch that they shine on themselves]*

PERSON 2 How about this one!? Am I bright enough now? Hmmm, actually I think I can go one better... Just a moment.

*[**PERSON 2** disappears again momentarily and re-appears with a really large, bright torch/lamp that they shine on themselves]*

PERSON 2 Okay, prepare yourselves. How about this one! Now I'm definitely bright enough for God.

PERSON 1 You've lost the plot.

PERSON 2 Right, I'm off.

PERSON 1 Where to?

PERSON 2 To stand on top of a hill. Bye!

THE BIG ACADEMY
BIG QUESTION #11
How am I supposed to tell people about Jesus?
NAME:
SPECIAL AGENT NAME:
CHECK IT OUT
Matthew 28:16-20
'Go to the world' –the whole world?!
BIG Story
Jesus told His disciples they (and also us) should be like salt and light in the world! Weird!
Matt 5: 13-16
Draw a really cool torch here...
What's the most exciting thing you've ever heard about?
Did you tell people about this or keep it a secret?
BONUS BIG QUESTION: Why doesn't God just tell everyone He exists + that He loves them? (then I wouldn't have to!)
What does it mean?
EVANGELISE
IF I DO THESE THINGS DO I STILL HAVE TO USE WORDS?
HOW CAN I 'SHOW' PEOPLE WHO JESUS IS + WHAT HE'S LIKE?
Decorate the people!
It's pretty cool that if I tell 2 people about Jesus and they each tell 2 people... and so on... soon LOADS of people will know!
What does salt do to food?
How can we be like salt in the world?
Ask your leader...
Have you ever told anyone about Jesus? How did it go?!
CHALLENGE!
IT'S AGAINST THE CLOCK...
Get your leader to time you!
2 MIN.
TICK TICK
Help our little chappie reach the top of the lighthouse!
SO... #11
How can I tell people about Jesus?
PRAY...
Ask God for His help to tell people about Jesus...
AMEN!
'Ready or not... Here we come!'

BIG Question #12

DO I BELIEVE?

The Song:

I BELIEVE

6 mins

You will need:

- 'What do you know?' quiz

Prepare an age appropriate 'General Knowledge' quiz. Potentially a picture quiz with cartoon characters/people they would know from the TV etc.

Run it as a quiz, in teams or as individuals, depending on your group size.

4-7 mins

Ask everyone to come up with one thing about themselves that is true (something that people don't really know) and one thing that is a lie. One at a time, get the children to tell the rest of the group the truth and the lie. Everyone then has to guess which one is true - they must choose what to believe.

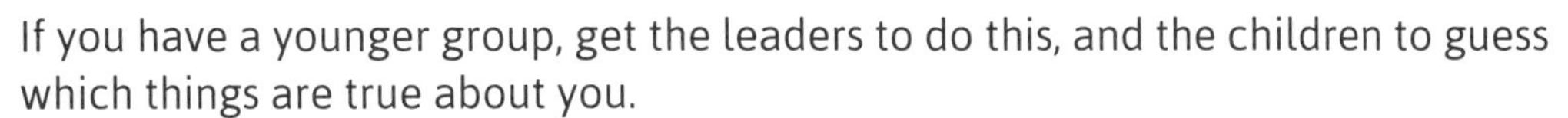

If you have a younger group, get the leaders to do this, and the children to guess which things are true about you.

Set the scene:

Tell the children that the BIG Question we're thinking about today is:
Do I Believe?

Tell the children that everyone has the choice as to whether or not they believe in Jesus. No one can make that choice for them.

10 mins

You will need:

- Story script (starting on *page 63*)
- Dressing-up
- Print-outs of the script for the children

This story will involve you splitting into three groups. Each group takes one part of the story of Saul. Each group then has to rehearse and perform their own dramatic interpretation of their part of the story for the other groups. Try to get them thinking of the sort of things each of the characters would say and the expressions on their faces. If you have some dressing-up clothes then that could also work well. If you have too many children for only three groups then hand out duplicates of parts of the story to any extra groups. If you don't have enough to split into three groups, do the three sections all together.

5 mins

You will need:

- *Welcome to the BIG Academy* album and facilities to play it.

Sing *I Believe* together (Track 12).

10-12 mins

You will need:

- An activity sheet copied for each child
- Pens/pencils
- Bibles

Go through the sheet - use it as a foundation for discussion. Allow the children to do the sheet however they would like to, but talk to them about the key questions as they are doing things.

7-10 mins

(Optional) **You will need:**

- Paper
- Scissors
- Sticky tape

Search YouTube (on the internet!) for, 'make a paper toy transformer'. There are a couple of videos that will show you how to make a very cool toy - you may need to pause it a few times.

6 mins

You will need:

- A means of taking photos and instantly printing them.
- A large piece of paper with big words, 'Academy Graduates', written at the top - Try and make it look like a college student photo board.

Take the children's photos, and invite them to stick their photo onto the 'Graduates board' if they do believe, and do want to follow Jesus, and do want to change the world for Him.

IMPORTANT EXTRA

This is the final session, and very much a commissioning time.

- Do these children want to graduate from the BIG Academy and get out there and change the world?
- Challenge them - if they do then get them to stick their photo up on the board.
- Give the children the option of taking their photo home to think about it, they can bring it back another time.

You could even have a 'graduation party' this week or another time with food/a bit of a ceremony. It might be good to get a church leader involved/some graduation hats/something to help the children realise that this is really exciting and they are really part of something BIG here...

So... do I believe?
I don't know... do you?

SAUL'S TRANSFORMATION (ACTS)

Saul's Transformation - Part One

Characters:
Saul, Saul's soldiers, Christians, Jesus, Narrator

- In the City of Jerusalem, there was once a man named Saul. He was an angry man; he was a fierce and ferocious man.
- Saul HATED Christians. He could not stand them. He wanted to see them all locked up and in prison... or dead!
- Saul would go from house to house, knocking on doors in order to find as many Christians as he could. Then he would throw them in a cold, damp prison, away from the rest of the world.
- One particular day, Saul decided to go to the City of Damascus to round up some more Christians. His plan was to bring them all back to Jerusalem and have them thrown in prison.
- Saul and his soldiers loaded themselves up with food and water and weapons and then set off on their journey.
- As they neared Damascus, a bright, bright light shone in front of Saul and a voice spoke out, "Saul, why are you persecuting me?" "Who are you Lord?" replied Saul. "I am Jesus. Now get up and go to the city of Damascus. I will then tell you what you must do."
- And so, Saul stood up, but he could not see a thing. He was blind.

Saul's Transformation - Part Two

Characters:
Saul, Saul's soldiers, Ananias, Disciples, Narrator

- It was now three days since Saul had met with Jesus on the road to Damascus and he was still blind and sat in a house in the City of Damascus.
- People would offer Saul food, but he didn't want to eat anything. People would offer Saul water, but he didn't want to drink anything. All that Saul did was to sit and pray. For three days he did this.
- After three days, Jesus sent a man named, Ananias, to go and pay Saul a visit. Ananias was a little anxious about this, as he'd heard a lot of bad things about Saul.
- Ananias laid his hands on Saul and Saul immediately received his sight.
- Saul was then baptised, he ate some food and he then went and spent some time with the disciples of Jesus and also taught in the synagogues.
- Saul had completely transformed. He was no longer the angry, fierce and ferocious man that he once was. He now loved others and wanted to tell everyone he met about Jesus.

Saul's Transformation - Part Three

Characters:
Saul, Jews, Disciples, Prison guard, Christians

- Saul had been transformed through his meeting with Jesus. He was once an angry, fierce and ferocious man who hated Christians, but now he loved others and wanted to tell everyone he met about Jesus.
- Because Saul was now a Christian, many of the Jewish people that he once spent time with (the people who wanted to get rid of the Christians) wanted to get rid of him. There was a plan to kill him!
- The Jewish people who wanted Saul dead kept a close watch on the city gates of Damascus, waiting for Saul to leave the City so that they could kill him. But, Saul had heard of their plan and some of the disciples lowered him in a basket through a hole in the city walls.
- Saul, who was now known as Paul, continued to tell people of the good news of Jesus and the church continued to grow and grow.
- Travelling around from town to town, Paul would tell people about Jesus everywhere he went and would also strengthen and encourage the churches that he met along the way.
- Paul was even thrown in prison for being a Christian and, a number of times, had to escape being killed by people who hated him.
- Paul, who was once an angry, fierce and ferocious man who hated Christians and Jesus, was transformed in the most miraculous way and was used by Jesus everywhere he went.

BIG QUESTION #12
Do I believe?
NAME:
SPECIAL AGENT NAME:
THE BIG ACADEMY
BIG Story
Saul was transformed from someone who hated Jesus (and people who followed Him) to someone who followed Jesus and told other people all about Him! CRAZY!
Acts
What's your favourite food?
Can you imagine NOT eating or drinking for 3 whole days? How do you think Saul felt (apart from hungry!)
Do you believe in...
1) The tooth fairy?
2) The Loch Ness Monster?
3) Father Christmas?
what about
4) Time travel?
Is it different when we say we believe in Jesus (to believing in these things?!)
CHECK IT OUT
Romans 10:9
fill in the blanks
If you say:
'________ is _______' and believe in your ________ then you will be ____________!
What does it mean?
FAITH
Why does Jesus want me to believe in Him?
Anananias and Saul both spoke with Jesus...
Can we speak with Jesus? Does He talk to us?
WHAT DO YOU BELIEVE?
Do you believe
• God made the world
• God loves everyone
• God sees and hears everything
• God sent Jesus to earth
• Jesus lived a perfect, fully human life
• Jesus died and came back to life to fix the messed up world
• Jesus went back to heaven but sent His Spirit to be with us
• The Spirit is with us and helps us to do good things in Jesus' name.
If you do believe all those things, that's super great... but there's more...
There's another question - So what?
Believing something doesn't necessarily make a difference, you have to DO too! For example: you might really need to sit down because your legs are tired. You might believe that a chair can hold your weight, but it doesn't help your tired legs unless you actually trust it and sit down!
For our belief in Jesus to mean something we need to DO things & trust Him that He will be with us, just like He said He would.
Check out James 2: 14-26.
CHALLENGE!
Wordsearch time (we know you love them!)
W F Q B P F E Y J B E K
C A M K I V O E A W S J
X I W T E L S L M R B O
H T F I F U L Q L L P E
W H L Q S V A L A O M Q
E E J E R A L U A P W I
B A N A N I A S D M P N
IT'S AGAINST THE CLOCK... Get your leader to time you!
2 MIN.
TICK TICK
believe
faith
Jesus
follow
Ananias
Paul
pray
BONUS BIG QUESTION:
Do I have to change if I believe in and follow Jesus?
SO... #8 Do you believe?
and will it make a difference to your life?
PRAY...
AMEN!
'I'm giving it everything I've got for You and the things I believe in.'

About Us

BIG Ministries love to celebrate God and have loads of fun doing it! They mainly do this by putting on events across the country (check out the website to see if there are any near you) as well as writing resources for churches to use with their children's groups and in all-age services. Get in touch if you think they could help you, or if you'd like to join them at an event!

t: 01527 556639
e: info@bigministries.co.uk
w: bigministries.co.uk

bigministriesuk (Twitter)
bigministriesuk (Facebook)